Cooking on Your Own

ALSO BY HENRY LEWIS CREEL

Cooking for One Is Fun

Cooking on Your Own

HENRY LEWIS CREEL

Foreword by Craig Claiborne

Times
BOOKS

Published by TIMES BOOKS, a division of
Quadrangle/The New York Times Book Co., Inc.
Three Park Avenue, New York, N.Y. 10016

Published simultaneously in Canada by
Fitzhenry & Whiteside, Ltd., Toronto

Library of Congress Cataloging in Publication Data

Creel, Henry Lewis.
Cooking on your own.

Includes index.
1. Cookery.   I. Title.
TX652.C79 1980   641.5   80-13108
ISBN 0-8129-0837-6

Manufactured in the United States of America

FOR

Craig, Pierre, and Ann

Foreword

It has long been my thesis that cooking is the greatest form of therapy. What other diversion can so neatly fulfill the needs of body and emotion as well?

And rarely have I known any more demonstrative of that thesis than Henry Lewis Creel.

Henry retired from professional life ten years ago, after thirty-five years as an executive with one of America's leading oil companies. Retirement for many people is exceedingly demanding. I have also never known anyone better able to meet those demands than Henry.

Cooking is, indeed, one of the major pleasures of his life. Now approaching his seventieth birthday and in excellent health, he spends a good portion of his time today in planning menus for himself, in food preparation preface to a meal (principally dinner), and in the actual cooking.

Not that cooking is his single pleasurable manner of passing time. Far from it. He is an avid reader, an enthusiastic movie- and theatre-goer, and he travels more each year than most non-professionals I know. Last year he spent weeks travelling around the world—alone—visiting such places as the markets in Hong Kong, the Taj Mahal in Agra, and the Topkapi in Istanbul, as well as several cities in Japan.

But it is my observation that the kitchen is his favorite domain and I can happily testify that he is a first-rate cook. I have had many meals in his presence and as far as I can recall have never tasted a failure that came from his gas range, which is situated in a handsome apartment in Manhattan.

Fortunately, Henry has never known considerable financial pressures. Yet this is one book that is based on economy for the simple reason that the author practices a frugality that even the most sparing, purse-watching Scot would marvel at. He delights in using inexpensive cuts of meat. Although there may be a few extravagances here and there, the only ones that come to mind have been cooked in his kitchen not only because they tasted good but because they could be cooked in a hurry. These would include such of today's luxuries as veal scallopine and shrimp, but even these he tends to use in limited amounts for any given recipe.

Speed, too, is also a happy factor in these recipes. The author is not a "fiddler" in the kitchen when it comes to food. That is to say he does not make each meal a tedious extravaganza, spending hours in preparing it. Far from it. He enjoys a drink or two before dinner, and he'd rather get his excellent act together in the kitchen, then go sit down for a nice quiet hour over a cocktail.

CRAIG CLAIBORNE
East Hampton, New York
December 1979

Foreword

It has long been my thesis that cooking is the greatest form of therapy. What other diversion can so neatly fulfill the needs of body and emotion as well?

And rarely have I known any more demonstrative of that thesis than Henry Lewis Creel.

Henry retired from professional life ten years ago, after thirty-five years as an executive with one of America's leading oil companies. Retirement for many people is exceedingly demanding. I have also never known anyone better able to meet those demands than Henry.

Cooking is, indeed, one of the major pleasures of his life. Now approaching his seventieth birthday and in excellent health, he spends a good portion of his time today in planning menus for himself, in food preparation preface to a meal (principally dinner), and in the actual cooking.

Not that cooking is his single pleasurable manner of passing time. Far from it. He is an avid reader, an enthusiastic movie- and theatre-goer, and he travels more each year than most non-professionals I know. Last year he spent weeks travelling around the world—alone—visiting such places as the markets in Hong Kong, the Taj Mahal in Agra, and the Topkapi in Istanbul, as well as several cities in Japan.

But it is my observation that the kitchen is his favorite domain and I can happily testify that he is a first-rate cook. I have had many meals in his presence and as far as I can recall have never tasted a failure that came from his gas range, which is situated in a handsome apartment in Manhattan.

Fortunately, Henry has never known considerable financial pressures. Yet this is one book that is based on economy for the simple reason that the author practices a frugality that even the most sparing, purse-watching Scot would marvel at. He delights in using inexpensive cuts of meat. Although there may be a few extravagances here and there, the only ones that come to mind have been cooked in his kitchen not only because they tasted good but because they could be cooked in a hurry. These would include such of today's luxuries as veal scallopine and shrimp, but even these he tends to use in limited amounts for any given recipe.

Speed, too, is also a happy factor in these recipes. The author is not a "fiddler" in the kitchen when it comes to food. That is to say he does not make each meal a tedious extravaganza, spending hours in preparing it. Far from it. He enjoys a drink or two before dinner, and he'd rather get his excellent act together in the kitchen, then go sit down for a nice quiet hour over a cocktail.

CRAIG CLAIBORNE
East Hampton, New York
December 1979

Contents

Contents

Introduction

I know that people might say that I am in a rut, continuing my thing of cooking for myself and setting down and accumulating the recipes that please me. I got into this habit in preparing *Cooking for One Is Fun* and I am still following it. I probably always will. Being in a rut isn't as bad as it sounds. It can mean that one has found a satisfying life-style.

Cooking recipes for one serving was a natural for me because I have lived alone for many years and I have enjoyed staying in and relishing my own home by cooking for myself and not having to go out for meals, most of all for dinner. I enjoy dressing comfortably and fixing my own evening meal. As a matter of fact, I find my own cooking of simple things superior to that of many restaurants, not necessarily because I am a better cook, but because I prepare what I want at the time—something I have thought about, marketed for, and worked up an appetite for. Whereas, at restaurants, I have to select from what the cook has to offer and that is not like having your own idea and following through with it. So I dine better and more comfortably at home. Many people living alone can do the same with a recipe, a little cooking skill, and an appetite.

Quickly let me point out that the idea of preparing one serving and not more is a valuable idea. It evolved a decade or so ago when I was gaining weight without trying or wanting to. I arrived at the point where I had to do something about it. I thought about it, observed others, and learned that many good cooks taste their food but refrain from consuming large quantities and certainly don't eat seconds. Thus came my temporary rule of always leaving something on my plate. In other words, I learned that it is the quantity of intake, qualified somewhat by calorific content, that determines the level of gain. I used my temporary rule by pausing in the middle of a meal and thinking. Invariably I decided that I was already sufficiently nourished and satisfied, and, with my objective in mind to lose weight, I would forego the remainder of the serving. I did lose weight but I rebelled at the waste and that led me to cooking just enough for one serving. I believe in never tempting myself by preparing an excess that I might go ahead and finish.

In order to have a file of recipes to guide me the second time around and in the future, I began a collection of these recipes for one serving, enjoying my kitchen, watching my weight, and economizing all at the same time. When I retired and purchased a typewriter, I found my collection of recipes readable and I used them in my kitchen long before I thought of publication.

Recipes for one serving have intrinsic qualities. They are more easily understood by occasional and amateur cooks, and non-cooks are even tempted to try. I have one anecdote applicable here. It concerns a letter I received from an acquaintance, a retired executive, who told me that he had observed in *Cooking for One Is Fun*, a recipe for *steak au poivre*, that he had tried it and found it very good, and that he was going to try *boeuf en daube* next. His wife added a note at the bottom of the letter saying that her husband had found the book and had started limited cooking, and she ended by saying: "I like that."

I consider recipes for one serving like building blocks. They can be doubled or trebled by watching the cooking times and seasonings. My advice is to study the recipe for one serving and boldly face the problem of preparing enough for two or three, tasting and watching carefully to avoid any pitfalls that may arise from exactly doubling or trebling a recipe built especially for one serving. I have been happy to hear from people saying that they have done just this. One letter from a retired couple in New Jersey said that since the children are now settled in their own homes and since they are now just two, they have often doubled the recipes for one serving and have enjoyed them.

My first cooking was aimed at creating the tastes and aromas of my youth: the soups (asparagus, corn, vegetable); country cured ham; fried chicken; chicken salad; real pimiento cheese; and others. (I haven't tried salt-rising light bread, but I used to love it.) Such were my kitchen encounters of the first kind.

Cooking on
Your Own

Later I went from Missouri to New York for graduate study, and, later still, to western Europe, and in these places I found an abundance of new tastes and aromas: fresh fish, ethnic foods, etc. Here was the inspiration for my kitchen encounters of the second kind.

Now I have reached a higher level of inspiration which almost miraculously comes to mind without strain. Now I frequently purchase something in the market that looks particularly appetizing, fresh, or well-marked. I take this item home, refrigerate it, and go on about my business, keeping the purchase in the back of my mind. Always, a way to prepare the new item comes to mind and I begin the trials on a new recipe for one serving.

I will never forsake some of the recipes in the home cooking category. They have a permanent place in my mind. Nor will I cease to emulate fish cookery of the east coast—where fresh fish is so readily available—French cuisine, Italian, Chinese, and others that I enjoy. But, frankly, it is rewarding to come up with a recipe somewhat original. There is always fun in a new taste and a new creation.

HENRY CREEL
New York
December 1979

Shopping for One

I have enjoyed cooking for myself over the years. It is fun and a comfort. Also, it becomes easier, the results are tastier, and the variety is more interesting as time goes on. I know the advantages, but I want to mention the disadvantages and how I have coped with them, because I know some thought and planning are needed to smooth out the problems and add to the enjoyment.

Simply stated, the problems, or disadvantages if you will, are all connected with supply. I refer to purchasing in small quantities and storing and preserving excesses for future use. I can say I have successfully solved these problems and I do not incur waste, nor am I forced to cook something just to get it out of the way. There is no secret solution. None at all. Success comes easily, however, with advance planning: a list for marketing, purchasing in exact quantities, or purchasing packages and carefully storing the excess. Storage includes proper refrigeration and freezing, sometimes cooking and refrigerating for use a few days later.

I plan for today with an eye for tomorrow and down the road as well. My list for current marketing includes the fresh ingredients for the next meal and often something to freeze for later, as I don't like to shop daily. And at the supermarket I fill the quota allowed me for passage through the express line with staples that store well on the shelf or in the refrigerator. I use my quota of ten or so and would rather go twice to the market than stand behind one of those family carts with a week's supply.

It has been a help to me to have a handy pad in the kitchen for jotting down staples and random inspirations as staples run out and as inspirations pop up. This pad goes with me to the market.

I am glad to find today a proliferation of so called bulk markets where I can pick out just what I need: a handful of green beans, two onions, three mushrooms, and whatever small quantities I re-

4 • Cooking on Your Own

quire for a certain recipe. This type of purchasing is undoubtedly more costly, but not as uneconomical as the waste involved in purchasing large packages.

I can't resist a venture into the supermarket, however, where I enjoy seeing what is available and where I may find inspiration because of the appeal of some item or items. The packages of fresh vegetables are always too large for one serving but the excess can be stored in the refrigerator. I always wrap items to be stored or bag them to keep out air and maintain freshness. I use see-through plastic wrap or bags and press out all the air possible before sealing or tying the package to be stored for later use.

Incidentally, I keep opened coffee in the refrigerator and I haven't used a bread box in years. I keep the bread wrapped tightly in its original wrapper, if it remains intact, and I refrigerate it for weeks with success.

Although I enjoy fresh herbs when available, or when I remember to list them and seek them out, I keep a large supply of dried herbs and spices because they keep well and are handy. To my mind, parsley especially is only parsley when it is fresh, and I keep a supply tightly sealed in a jar with a screw top and refrigerated.

Meat is treated similarly in my kitchen. I sometimes buy just the quarter pound of veal or whatever to fit the recipe at hand, but more frequently I purchase a package of more than one serving at the supermarket. I use more breast of chicken than anything, because it is the best value and because it is so adaptable to many methods of preparation. Since the packages of chicken breasts in the markets usually include at least two breasts and I use half a breast for one serving, I freeze the halves of chicken breast in individual packages using wax paper or foil—I prefer the wax paper because of its transparency. Similarly, I cut the ground meat packages in quarter-pound portions and wrap them in wax paper and freeze them. Also, I wrap chops or small steaks and freeze them until required. They keep well and the freezing does not damage the taste enough to risk spoiling when unfrozen in the refrigerator. I freeze all meats not to be consumed immediately and I defrost them in the refrigerator, starting usually on the morning of the day of the dinner.

There are dishes that are better aged a day or so. These are the spiced dishes—stews, chili, ragout, goulash, and others. I prepare such a dish frequently before the day of a heavy schedule and enjoy leftovers and more time for the other activity on the following day. This is the usual procedure for me on Tuesdays, because I like to see Broadway shows at Wednesday matinees, and I can have part of the cooking finished when I arrive home from the theater late on matinee days. Of course I double the recipes for one serving and plan for enough for a second meal. There are other dishes that keep well for another day under refrigeration. I keep excess vegetables for salads and soups the next day, and cold chicken, steak, lamb, and other meats make a delightful lunch on the day after. I remember four or five decades or so ago hearing Aunt Sallie telling a neighbor that she was having cold lamb for lunch, and I still remember that both of us were impressed.

I do use leftovers when I double or triple a recipe for one serving in the interest of saving time the next day or with the foresight of planning a portion of the recipe for use in a different way. For example, I have doubled the chili recipes frequently. Then, the first day, I have chili with garnishes of one or several of the following: chopped onion, chopped green pepper, shredded lettuce, or chopped celery; and, on the second day, I use the leftover chili in another presentation: in a stuffed green pepper, in a grits ring, or over corn bread or a baked potato. Leftovers can be lightly disguised and enjoyed. I dislike wasting them, but I never finish them just to avoid waste. Someone once advised wisely not to act as a garbage can. I certainly agree and say: Find a use, maybe the next day.

In the interest of keeping my weight down and maintaining comfort I hold to small servings. They do this in many of the finest restaurants of France and Italy. I always suspect the establishment that heaps food on a plate. A small serving, certainly a small serving at the start, is a must. I also feel strongly on the subject of over-seasoning, particularly with the most common seasonings like salt, mustard, tarragon, and garlic, and even with the less common seasonings that are not as pronounced. It is a pitfall to become addicted to lots of salt. It is reportedly not healthy for most people and it obscures delicate flavors. I believe in using salt, mustard, etc., carefully and on the low side and letting the flavor of the food be complimented, not concealed. I like imported mustard, but too much on the pastrami makes the pastrami taste just like mustard.

I love cooking for the budding appetite of the moment and doing it with basic, fresh ingredients proportioned to one serving. My thing concerns finding, testing, and preserving recipes for one serving for my future use and for others who can find pleasure where I have. Recipes and their variations are unlimited and I am glad of that. I enjoy trying new dishes all the time and I always keep an eye out for the next challenge. I recommend cooking different, new, and varied dishes regularly. When I hear some people complain of cooking as a chore, I know that these unfortunates are stuck on meat and potatoes, a combination that allows only a limited number of dishes. With a little variety, the possibilities are there for simple, good, varied meals from any kitchen.

Equipping a Kitchen for One

What I use in my kitchen is special to me and I believe the feeling is universal among those who love to work in the kitchen. It may be very old equipment like the bent and scarred old kitchen spoon I cherish, the same one I remember many decades ago in my mother's kitchen, an article that would be thrown out quickly by anyone not attached to it by sentiment. Not me. I have used the spoon many years and I will continue to use it until it finally wears away. Then there is the large ladle-type spoon, 2½ by 2 inches, that was used when I was a child and there was no homogenized milk available. It served to skim the cream from the milk that had been settled in a white, enameled, flat pan. This cream provided a whipped cream dessert for a spoiled son. I smile contentedly as I continue to skim liquids with this spoon, and it is just the thing for dishing out soups and stews that need to be served with a flavorful sauce. Also, I have and use a pair of small spoons that came with a mustard set, I believe, years ago. They are very useful for extracting relish, preserves, or mustard from small-mouthed glass containers or for scraping tomato paste from those small cans. Of course the large slotted spoon is indispensable for serving vegetables from the water in which they were cooked. There are also the long-handled small spoon, the melon cutter, and the baby spoon in the sugar. But the most used in my kitchen are the old kitchen spoon and the ladle.

As far as knives are concerned I frequently find myself sparing my 10-inch stainless steel chef's knife from France, which is perfect for chopping vegetables by holding the tip in one hand and the handle in the other. I use the 10-inch from time to time, but, for small quantities of chopped ingredients for a single serving, I normally use the 4-inch paring knife which goes in the dishwasher. It serves the purpose well for small quantities and I keep it sharp by

7

occasional passes through the sharpener attachment on the can opener. I am sure a professional chef would never dream of using a paring knife to such an extent, but for me it works well and quickly. Indispensable to my kitchen cutting is the vegetable or potato peeler used not only for peeling potatoes but also for scraping carrots and peeling asparagus, apples, turnips, etc. Also, the pointed end of the peeler is useful not only for taking eyes out of potatoes and blemishes out of various and sundry vegetables but for removing the green stems from strawberries and the seeds from cherries. Added too is the gadget on the other end of the peeler that will cut julienne shapes.

There are five forks that I use in my kitchen, but I could do without all but one of them. The five vary in size from the long 11½-inch two-prong fork for manipulating larger items of food; to the 8¼-inch four-prong silver fork that I use to toss salad, coleslaw, etc., with its matching spoon; to the regular four-prong 6-inch salad fork, one of a set, which I always use to beat eggs; to the smallest fork, a two-prong 5½-inch sterling silver fork inherited from Aunt Sallie that is just right for spearing olives out of narrow-necked bottles, for those who require such fruit in their martini. The last of my forks and the one that is used most frequently is a three-prong, narrow, 5½-inch fondue fork. I know it is intended to spear bits of bread to dip in melted cheese or bits of meat to dip and cook in hot liquid, but I use the fondue fork for almost everything. It is narrow, light, long, and doesn't get in the way. It is useful, and, as I indicated above, I could give up all the other forks rather than part with the fondue fork. I bought the fork originally, just one fork, to spear small and medium beets from boiling water and to hold them for peeling while still hot. From that chore the multiple uses developed naturally.

There is another bit of cutting I do with an instrument meant for another use, but used by me for one chore only: shelling shrimp. I love preparing and eating shrimp and I keep the Hoffritz 4-inch fingernail scissors sheathed in the utility drawer for that one purpose. The small scissors are just right for cutting along the back of the shrimp from head to tail and deep enough to open the vein to be discarded under a stream of cold water. And the shell peels off easily, taking the legs from the underside with it. It is so much easier with the small nail scissors.

Cooking pots and pans of enameled iron are the usual aids in my kitchen and they are mostly made in Belgium and carry the trademark Le Creuset. The most used articles are casseroles with covers. Although I maintain an assortment of them in various sizes, the ones that I use most frequently are 6¼ inches in diameter by about 2½ inches deep, weighing about 2½ pounds each with cover. This size is perfect for cooking small quantities and for storing cooked foods in the refrigerator. Another useful pot is the 5-inch size. This I use for making sauces (cheese sauce, tomato sauce) in advance and covering until serving time when reheating can be done quickly over a Flame-Tamer. The latter I use often to cut down the heat and distribute it evenly over the bottoms of pots and pans. For example, I like dishes that are cooked covered tightly over very low heat with little or no liquid added. The Flame-Tamer comes in handy here.

Au gratin dishes I use for baking and passing under the broiler quickly before serving to brown the top. My favorite and most used size is the 6¼-inch round Le Creuset. This is just right for six baked shrimp Italian-style. I use the 6- by 8-inch oval au gratin dish for eight shrimp. These two are practical for many dishes of one serving or two. I seldom use the larger au gratins.

My favorite saucepan is 6¼ inches in diameter with cover, also made in Belgium, and the 5-inch saucepan without cover. Also I use the double Discoware pan with top that can be used separately as a small skillet.

My skillets are of the same material and I find the 9-inch skillet most often satisfactory for my recipes, although I occasionally use the 7-inch size. When there is a fillet of flounder or whatever of larger area I use the 11-inch skillet to advantage. It also serves well for browning chicken and other meats that should be cooked segregated, untouching.

I have a large copper stockpot 8¼ inches in diameter by 7 inches in depth, which I use occasionally for soup and now and then for boiling a small lobster. The copper pot replaces the old aluminum pot, 8½ inches by 5½ inches, which I purchased immediately after acquiring my first kitchen in St. Louis at the beginning of my business career. I was in such a hurry because I love vegetable soup and I couldn't wait to buy my own soup bone and vegetables and make my own pot of vegetable soup home-style. Needless to say, with my enthusiasm I collected so many vegetables that my new aluminum pot was entirely inadequate. I still keep this pot and fill it with water for boiling corn on the cob or for cooking spaghetti and other pasta. The pot is light and easily handled and goes in the dishwasher comfortably, and I always smile when I use it, recalling the soup containment problem at its initiation.

I use another aluminum pan frequently—my 4½-inch pie pan, just right for individual pies. For baking corn muffins, flan, custard, and other small items, I maintain a battery of Pyrex muffin cups. The 3¾-inch size I find most useful.

I became impressed with a food mill and puréed vegetables when I was in Casablanca toward the end of World War II. There, a captain friend invited me to a treat, a home-cooked meal, in the room of his French girlfriend, a Parisian refugee, who had kitchen privileges with her rented room. On one trip down the long hall from the kitchen to her front room she brought *soupe de chou,* or cabbage soup, which was a peasant dish but delightful after the fare at the officer's mess. So, of course, I asked how she did it and was told that the cooked, seasoned cabbage was passed through a "passoir" which is French for sieve, or a food mill. On my return to the United States a few months later, the first thing I bought was a food mill, a container with sieve-like holes in the bottom and a crank with rotor blade to push the cooked food through into a purée. I bought this gadget at a hardware store even before my kitchen was ready in my new apartment, and I still use it. The job of puréeing can be done much more quickly and efficiently in the food processor, which I always use for larger quantities and when I plan several different operations with the processor before it is stored in the dishwasher. However, for small quantities I often turn to the hand-operated food mill.

The food processor is excellent also for making dough for pies, biscuits, etc., but again I frequently fall back to the primitive style and use a small bowl and fingertips when I want three biscuits or an individual pie crust for a four-inch pie. I place the flour in a 5½-inch soup bowl which is about 2 inches deep, add the shortening, and knead with just the tips of the fingers. Tips, I emphasize, so there is less waste in washing the hand when some mixture sticks as it always will. Another innovation when working with small quantities is that I do without a breadboard and rolling pin.

Instead, I flour wax paper on the kitchen counter and roll out the dough with a tin can, 2 inches by 3¾ inches, a can especially prepared for the purpose by cutting out and discarding the ends. And I can cut out biscuits by pressing an open end into the dough. It works. Strange? No. I have seen cut out baking powder cans used for biscuit and cookie cutters in many aromatic home kitchens. And I doubt it is just an old Missouri custom.

I have set aside my Chemex coffee-maker, which I used for many years, in favor of the Mr. Coffee machine, as it is fast and, if you know how to use it, efficient. I find it necessary, with my model of Mr. Coffee, to pour the coffee through for a second go at the coffee grounds which remain dry in part after the original drip-through of water. Then I have two or three good cups of strong coffee. The nine-cup percolator remains on the shelf unless coffee-drinking guests arrive.

Well-cooked food is one thing to strive for, but I don't believe in neglecting taste in its presentation. I am happy to have inherited fine china and silver and I take joy in properly setting the table with the best for every meal. This ceremony I recommend. It is an extension of the "fun" you can have in your own kitchen and a life-style to be relished.

One habit in my kitchen has become a standard procedure for me and a must. It has to do with washing the dishes and cleaning up. I used to fret about having to wash the soap out of a sponge before using it to wipe up and dry the counter and other areas, and I found it time-saving and efficient to use two sponges: one always soaped and the other never soaped. This means, if you choose the correct sponge, that you don't have to rinse and rinse to wash out the soap when you don't want it and have need only for a sponge to dry a surface. In my kitchen, the sponge without soap is always on the right and the sponge with soap is on the left. I was telling this to a former neighbor of mine, the late food editor of a national magazine, thinking that this habit of mine would be amusing to her. I was expecting a laugh when she asked if she could quote me in her next column. And she did publish the idea, adding that sponges of two colors would be appropriate: one color for the clean sponge and another color for the sponge with soap. Now I use two colors too—but I still keep the no-soap sponge on the right.

Appetizers

Nothing can beat a delicate and well-prepared appetizer as an introduction to an enjoyable meal. It can be as simple and exotic as an Avocado Salad, Poireau Vinaigrette, or a delicious Oyster Cocktail.

AVOCADO SALAD

1 small, ripe avocado	Salt to taste
1 scallion, minced	1 teaspoon lemon juice
1 tablespoon diced pimiento	2 shakes paprika

1. Cut the avocado into halves and remove the seed.
2. Scoop out the flesh of the avocado with a melon ball scoop or small spoon and put it in a small mixing bowl. Add the scallion, pimiento, salt, and lemon juice. Mix well.
3. Discard one half shell and stuff the other half shell with the avocado mixture. Sprinkle with the paprika, cover, and refrigerate until serving time.

Note: This can be served either as a first course or as a salad. To serve as a salad, turn the refrigerated mixture out on a lettuce leaf, pouring a little French dressing over it, if desired.

GUACAMOLE

1 ripe avocado, peeled and seeded	1 small onion, peeled
Salt and freshly ground black pepper to taste	1 tablespoon chopped pimiento
	Paprika
1 teaspoon lemon juice, or to taste	Sliced stuffed olives (optional)

Place all ingredients, except the paprika and stuffed olives in the container of a food processor. Turn the motor on and off several times for a second at a time. Push the ingredients down the sides of the container with a narrow spatula. (Do this with the motor off, of course.) Turn the motor on and off one more time and then remove the guacamole to a small bowl. Cover and refrigerate until serving time. When you are ready to serve, remove the guacamole from the refrigerator, uncover it, sprinkle the top with paprika, and garnish with sliced stuffed olives, if desired. Serve with potato chips, tortilla chips, or crackers.

Note: This recipe can be prepared without using the food processor. Simply mash the avocado flesh with a fork, and then add to it the finely minced onion and pimiento. Mix well. Then add the lemon juice and salt and pepper and mix well again. Refrigerate and garnish as explained above.

CELERY ROOT REMOULADE

1 very small celery root, or several thin slices of a pared celery root	½ teaspoon Dijon mustard
	½ teaspoon lemon juice, or to taste
1 tablespoon mayonnaise	

1. Using a sharp, heavy knife, cut the thin slices of celery root into the thinnest possible strips. These should look like toothpicks or smaller.

2. Combine the mayonnaise, mustard, and lemon juice. Mix well and taste. You may want to add more lemon juice.
3. Add the thin strips of celery root to the mayonnaise mixture and combine well. Cover tightly and refrigerate until serving time.

POIREAU VINAIGRETTE

This is an excellent first course before a rich hot entrée.

1 large or 2 small leeks, trimmed and pared	Chopped greens
Water	Vinaigrette sauce, French dressing, or lemon and oil

1. Slice the trimmed leek lengthwise. Run under cool water to remove all sand particles.
2. Tie the leek into its original shape, using kitchen string. Put the reshaped leek into a small saucepan and cover with water. Bring to a boil, lower the heat to simmer, and cook until tender. When cooked, drain the leek, snip off the string, and allow to cool.
3. Serve on a bed of chopped greens with vinaigrette sauce, French dressing, or an oil and lemon dressing.

OYSTER COCKTAIL—1

6 shucked oysters	1 teaspoon lemon juice
2 tablespoons ketchup	5 drained capers (optional)
1 tablespoon plus 1 teaspoon prepared horseradish, or less	1 tablespoon shredded lettuce

1. Drain the oysters in a sieve and discard their liquid.
2. Mix together the ketchup, horseradish, lemon juice, and capers, if used.
3. Line the bottom of a cocktail glass with the shredded lettuce. Put the drained oysters on the lettuce. Smother the oysters with the sauce and refrigerate until serving time.

Note: Prepare this no more than an hour in advance.

OYSTER COCKTAIL—2

4 shucked oysters
2 tablespoons prepared horseradish
2 tablespoons ketchup

Lemon juice to taste (optional)
1 teaspoon finely chopped green pepper
Shredded lettuce

1. Drain the oysters in a sieve and discard their liquid.
2. In a small bowl, mix the horseradish and ketchup together. Add the lemon juice and green pepper, if desired.
3. Line the bottom of a cocktail glass with the shredded lettuce. Arrange the drained oysters over the lettuce. Pour the sauce over the oysters, and chill until ready to serve. Serve with crackers, if desired.

SHRIMP COCKTAIL

2 tablespoons ketchup
1 tablespoon prepared horseradish
1 cornichon, minced (optional)
1 teaspoon lemon juice

Freshly ground black pepper
Shredded lettuce
6 or more shelled and deveined cooked shrimp
Lemon wedges (optional)

1. Put the ketchup, horseradish, minced cornichon, if desired, lemon juice, and black pepper to taste in a small jar with tight-fitting lid. Shake vigorously and refrigerate.
2. At serving time, line the bottom of a cocktail glass with the shredded lettuce. Put the shrimp on top of the lettuce. Shake the dressing again and pour it over the shrimp. Serve with lemon wedges, if desired.

Soups

Soup is the perfect food for any occasion. It makes a warm and satisfying meal by itself, it fits in well with salads and sandwiches, and serves as a delicious first course at a more elaborate meal. Whether you choose a light Oxtail Soup, a heavy Navy Bean Soup with Ham, or one of the tasty fish soups or chowders offered here, you are sure to enjoy.

COLD CUCUMBER AND AVOCADO SOUP ADELE

1 small cucumber, peeled, seeded, and cut into small lengths
1 small avocado, peeled and cut into small pieces
1 small white onion, peeled and sliced

1 tablespoon Worcestershire sauce
   Juice of ½ lemon
   Salt and freshly ground black pepper
½ cup chicken broth
¼ cup light or heavy cream (optional)

1. Put the cucumber, avocado, and onion in the container of a blender or food processor. Blend for 1 minute.
2. Season the soup with the Worcestershire sauce, lemon juice, and salt and pepper to taste. Add the chicken broth. Scrape down the sides of the blender container and blend the soup again briefly. Taste for seasoning, and correct, if necessary. Add the cream, if desired, and blend briefly. Refrigerate for at least ½ hour before serving.

CORN AND CRABMEAT SOUP

This can be prepared at the very last minute.

½ cup chicken broth
½ cup cream-style corn
2 teaspoons cornstarch
2 teaspoons water

Salt to taste
½ cup crabmeat, picked over and
flaked

1. Bring the chicken broth to a boil and add the creamed corn. Stir to mix well.
2. In a cup, dissolve the cornstarch in the water. Add the mixture to the soup and stir until the soup begins to thicken.
3. Add salt to taste and the crabmeat. Stir and heat to a boil, but do not boil. Serve immediately.

TWENTY-MINUTE CHICKEN AND TOMATO SOUP

1 small onion, peeled and thinly sliced
1 small potato, peeled and sliced
½ chicken breast (about 4 or 5 ounces), skinned, boned, and cubed

Salt and freshly ground black pepper
Tomato juice

1. Put the onion slices in the bottom of a small heavy pot with a cover. Layer the potato slices over the onion slices, and top with the chicken cubes. Sprinkle with salt and pepper to taste. Pour over tomato juice to cover all of the ingredients.
2. Bring to a boil, cover the pot, and lower the heat to simmer. Cook for 20 minutes, stirring occasionally. Serve hot.

CHICKEN-CORN SOUP

½ chicken breast with skin removed, or 4 or 5 ounces of chicken meat
¼ teaspoon thyme
¼ bay leaf
1 small carrot, trimmed, scraped, washed, and diced
1 small white onion, peeled and chopped
1 clove garlic, crushed
Chicken broth
Salt and freshly ground black pepper
1 fresh, uncooked ear of corn, shucked
2 teaspoons flour
2 teaspoons water

1. Put the chicken, thyme, bay leaf, carrot, onion, and garlic in a small heavy pot with a cover. Pour in enough chicken broth to cover the ingredients. Add salt and pepper to taste.
2. Bring to a boil, cover, reduce the heat, and simmer for 50 minutes, stirring occasionally. Remove the chicken and let it cool. Then cut it into bite-sized pieces.
3. Cut the kernels from the corn and add them to the broth. Bring to a boil and cover the pot. Turn off the heat and let the soup set.
4. At serving time, add the cut-up chicken to the soup and heat thoroughly. If desired, thicken the soup to taste with the flour and water mixture. Serve with crackers or toast.

FISH SOUP—1

1 teaspoon vegetable oil
¼ cup finely chopped onion
1 small clove garlic, peeled and chopped
1 tablespoon minced shallot
1 teaspoon flour
¼ cup canned tomatoes
1 8-ounce bottle clam juice
¼ cup dry white wine
¼ pound skinless and boneless white fish, such as halibut, striped bass, cod, or flounder, cut into ½-inch pieces
5 shelled and deveined shrimp
Salt and freshly ground black pepper
Pinch saffron (optional)
¼ teaspoon Pernod (optional)

1. Heat the oil in a heavy saucepan or small kettle. Add the onion and cook, stirring, until the onion is wilted, about 1 minute. Add the garlic and shallot and stir.
2. Sprinkle the vegetables with the flour and stir to coat.
3. Add the tomatoes, clam juice, and wine. Mix well and cook for 15 minutes, over medium heat, stirring occasionally.
4. Add the fish and shrimp. Season with salt and pepper to taste and add the saffron, if desired. Simmer for 15 minutes. Stir in the Pernod, if desired, and serve hot.

Note: Lobster and other fish may also be used in this recipe. Water, chicken broth, or fish stock (made with fish bones, skin, and pieces of fish simmered in water) can replace the clam broth.

FISH SOUP—2

2 tablespoons olive oil	¼ teaspoon saffron
1 clove garlic, peeled and finely minced	Salt and freshly ground black pepper
1 small onion, peeled and chopped	½ cup dry white wine
1 leek, trimmed, washed, and cut into 1-inch slices	½ cup fish stock, water or chicken broth
¼ cup chopped celery	¼ cup peeled, diced potato
¼ cup chopped carrot	¼ to ½ pound firm white-fleshed fish, such as cod or striped bass
¼ cup chopped green pepper	¼ cup cream
Pinch of dried thyme	Chopped parsley for garnish
1 bay leaf	

1. Heat the oil in a heavy casserole or kettle with a cover. Add the garlic and onion and sauté for about 1 minute.
2. Add the leek, celery, carrot, green pepper, thyme, bay leaf, saffron, and salt and pepper to taste. Stir well and cook for 1 minute.
3. Add the wine and stock, stir again, cover, and cook for 5 minutes.
4. Add the potatoes, cover, and cook for about 10 minutes.
5. Add the fish, stir, and cook for another 5 minutes.
6. Add the cream and bring the soup just to the boil. Serve hot, topped with the parsley.

LOBSTER SOUP

2 teaspoons butter
2 teaspoons flour
⅔ cup chicken broth
Meat from 1 boiled lobster
(see recipe page 151)

Salt and cayenne pepper
1 tablespoon cream
1 tablespoon sherry
Hot cooked rice (optional)

1. Melt the butter in a small heavy pot with a cover. Sprinkle the flour over the melted butter and cook, stirring, for about 1 minute. Quickly add the chicken broth and stir with a wire whisk until the soup begins to thicken. Add the lobster meat and mix well.
2. Season the soup with salt and cayenne to taste. Cover and keep warm.
3. At serving time, stir in the cream and then the sherry. Serve the soup hot over cooked rice, if desired.

SHRIMP SOUP

¼ pound or 6 medium-sized shrimp
1 tablespoon butter
1 small onion, peeled and finely chopped
1 small carrot, trimmed, scraped, washed, and thinly sliced
¼ teaspoon thyme
½ bay leaf
1 teaspoon chopped parsley

1 stalk celery, pared and finely chopped
½ cup dry white wine
2 tablespoons tomato purée
¼ teaspoon dried tarragon
1 clove garlic, peeled and crushed
Salt and freshly ground black pepper
1 cup chicken broth
½ teaspoon Pernod (optional)

1. Using a scissors, cut through the back shell of the shrimp into the flesh. Peel off the shell and wash the shrimp under cold running water to remove the exposed black vein. Set the shrimp aside.

2. Melt the butter in a heavy saucepan. Add the onion, carrot, thyme, bay leaf, parsley, and celery. Stir well and cook for 2 minutes.
3. Add the wine, tomato purée, tarragon, garlic, and salt and pepper to taste to the saucepan. Mix well. Add the chicken broth and mix again.
4. Bring to a boil, lower the heat, and simmer for 10 minutes, or until the vegetables are partially cooked but still firm. Add the prepared shrimp and simmer for no more than 3 minutes. Stir in the Pernod, if desired, and serve hot.

OYSTER CHOWDER

2 tablespoons butter
2 tablespoons chopped onion
½ cup chopped celery
1 small carrot, trimmed, scraped, washed, and chopped
½ cup peeled and diced potato
½ cup boiling water or chicken broth

Salt and freshly ground black pepper
6 shucked oysters with their liquid
¼ cup cream
Chopped parsley for garnish

1. Melt 1 tablespoon of butter in a skillet. Add the onion and celery and sauté for 1 minute. Add the carrot and potato and stir well. Pour in the boiling water, stir again, and simmer for 20 minutes, or until the vegetables are tender but not mushy. Season the soup with salt and pepper to taste and set aside.
2. Melt the remaining tablespoon of butter in a saucepan with a cover. Add the oysters and their liquid. Cover and cook over low heat for 2 minutes.
3. Stir the cream into the vegetables and combine this mixture with the oysters. Taste for seasoning, adding more salt and pepper, if necessary. Serve hot, garnished with the chopped parsley.

OYSTER STEW

1 tablespoon butter
6 to 8 oysters with their liquid
½ cup milk
1 tablespoon light cream

Salt
Paprika
Chopped parsley for garnish

Put the butter, oysters with their liquid, milk, cream, and salt and paprika to taste in the top of a double boiler. Heat the stew over simmering water until it just begins to bubble around the edges. Serve in a hot bowl, garnished with the chopped parsley.

SCALLOP-CORN CHOWDER

½ cup bay or sea scallops
2 teaspoons butter
1 small onion, peeled and thinly sliced
1 small potato, peeled and diced
1 8½-ounce can cream-style corn

1 teaspoon Worcestershire sauce
Salt and freshly ground black pepper
½ cup milk
Chopped parsley for garnish

1. Wash and pat the scallops dry with paper towels. If sea scallops are used, cut them in quarters. Bay scallops can be left whole.
2. Melt the butter in a heavy saucepan. When it is very hot, but not burning, add the sliced onion. Stir the onion slices to break them into rings. Cook for 1 minute.
3. Add the potato and stir and cook for 2 minutes more. Do not let the vegetables burn.
4. Pour in the creamed corn and stir to mix well. Season with the Worcestershire sauce and salt and pepper to taste. Blend well and cook for 2 minutes more.
5. Stir in the milk and then the scallops. Bring just to the boil, but do not boil. Serve hot, garnished with the chopped parsley and an additional bit of freshly ground black pepper, if desired.

CREAM OF CELERY SOUP

2 stalks celery, washed and trimmed
2 cups chicken broth
1 slice (about 2 ounces) cooked ham, cut into cubes

1 small onion, peeled and chopped
½ teaspoon dried thyme
Salt and freshly ground black pepper
2 tablespoons cream

1. Cut the celery into long lengthwise strips and slice the strips into small cubes. Put the celery, broth, ham, onion, thyme and salt and pepper to taste in a saucepan. Bring to a boil, lower the heat, and simmer until the celery is tender, about 30 minutes. Set the soup aside to cool.
2. Purée the soup in a food mill, blender, or food processor and refrigerate, covered, until serving time.
3. A few minutes before serving, return the soup to the saucepan and heat just to the boiling point. Taste for seasonings and add more salt and pepper, if necessary. Stir in the cream and return to the boiling point again, but do not let the soup boil. Serve hot.

SPLIT PEA AND HAM SOUP

⅓ cup dried split peas, washed and drained
2 ounces country-cured ham, diced
1 small onion, peeled and sliced

1 small carrot, trimmed, scraped, washed, and sliced
2 cups water
2 tablespoons cream
Salt and freshly ground black pepper (optional)

1. Put all the ingredients except the cream in a small heavy pot with a cover. Bring to a boil, lower the heat, and simmer for two hours, stirring occasionally.
2. Test the peas for doneness and taste the soup for seasonings. Add salt and pepper, if desired. Stir in the cream and serve the soup hot.

PEA SOUP WITH FRANKFURTERS

1 8½-ounce can LeSuer peas
1 cup College Inn beef broth
2 tablespoons heavy cream

3 frankfurters, cut into ¼-inch
   slices
   Salt and freshly ground black
   pepper

1. Purée the peas and their liquid in a food processor, blender, or food mill.
2. Pour the puréed peas, the beef broth, and cream into a small heavy saucepan. Bring the soup to a simmer.
3. Season the soup with salt and pepper to taste. (A more than generous amount of black pepper is very good.)
4. Add the frankfurter slices to the soup and simmer for 15 minutes. Serve hot.

ROMAN BEAN AND PASTA SOUP

¼ cup navy beans, washed and
   drained
1 13½-ounce can chicken broth,
   or about 2 cups homemade
   chicken broth
1 small onion, peeled and thinly
   sliced
1 small carrot, trimmed, scraped,
   washed, and thinly sliced

1 clove garlic, peeled and
   quartered
1½ ounces cooked ham, chopped
   Salt
   Crushed red pepper flakes
1 ounce spaghetti, or other pasta,
   in 1-inch pieces
½ teaspoon olive oil
   Freshly ground black pepper
   (optional)

1. Put the beans, chicken broth, onion, carrot, garlic, ham, and salt and crushed red pepper flakes to taste in a heavy saucepan with a cover. Bring to a boil, stirring occasionally. Cover, lower the heat, and simmer for about 1 hour, or until the beans are tender but not mushy.

2. Add the pasta and bring to a boil again. Cook, covered, for 10 minutes, or until the pasta is just tender.
3. Serve hot in a warm soup plate. Sprinkle the soup with the olive oil and black pepper, if desired.

NAVY BEAN SOUP WITH HAM

This hearty soup ages well, so it can be made the day before you want to serve it. A good pickle relish and some crackers complement it very well.

¼ cup navy beans, washed and drained
1 small onion, peeled and chopped
2 ounces ham (preferably country-cured), diced
2 tablespoons tomato sauce
4 cups water
Salt
Freshly ground black pepper

1. Put the beans, onion, ham, tomato sauce, and 2 cups of water in a heavy saucepan with a cover. Add a little salt and a generous amount of pepper. (Do not add too much salt at the beginning because the ham may be very salty.)
2. Bring to a boil, cover, reduce the heat, and simmer for several hours, or until the beans are thoroughly cooked. Add the remaining 2 cups of water a little at a time as the soup cooks. Just before the soup is done, test for seasonings and add more salt and pepper, if necessary.
3. Serve piping hot.

QUICK BEAN SOUP

1 teaspoon vegetable oil
⅓ cup chopped ham
1 tablespoon chopped onion
2 tablespoons chopped green
   pepper
1 8-ounce can whole tomatoes
½ cup water

1 teaspoon brown sugar
1 teaspoon vinegar
   Salt and freshly ground black
   pepper
½ cup canned baked beans,
   coarsely mashed

1. Heat the oil in a small heavy pot. Add the ham, onion, and green pepper and cook, stirring frequently, for about 4 minutes over medium heat.
2. Add the tomatoes, water, brown sugar, vinegar, and salt and pepper to taste. Cook for 10 minutes, stirring once. Remove from the heat.
3. At serving time, add the beans and bring the soup to a boil. Heat through and serve hot.

ZUCCHINI AND CARROT SOUP

1 medium-sized zucchini
2 medium-sized carrots
1 small onion
   Pinch of thyme
   Pinch of oregano
2 cups water

   Salt and freshly ground black
   pepper
½ cup milk or cream
¼ teaspoon Worcestershire sauce
1 teaspoon ketchup (optional)

1. Cut the ends off the zucchini and carrots and scrape, wash, and slice the vegetables. Peel and slice the onion.
2. Put the zucchini, carrots, onion, thyme, oregano, and water into a small heavy saucepan. Add salt and pepper to taste. Bring to a boil, reduce the heat, and simmer until the vegetables are tender.

3. Using a food processor, blender, or food mill, purée the vegetables and their liquid. Return to the saucepan and set aside until serving time.
4. At serving time, bring the soup to a simmer and add the milk, Worcestershire sauce, and ketchup, if desired. Serve hot.

OXTAIL SOUP

4 or 5 thin pieces of oxtail, 1½ inches long
Water to cover
Salt and freshly ground black pepper
1 carrot, trimmed, scraped, washed, and finely chopped

1 onion, peeled and chopped
1 stalk celery, trimmed, washed, and chopped
5 cherry tomatoes, washed and halved, or an equal amount of fresh or canned tomatoes (about ⅓ cup)

1. Put the oxtail pieces in a medium-sized saucepan with a cover. Add water to the pan, filling it to ½ inch of the top of the pan.
2. Add one-half teaspoon salt and black pepper to taste. Bring to a boil, cover, lower the heat, and simmer for 3 hours, stirring occasionally.
3. Pour the soup through a sieve into a bowl. Put the soup in the refrigerator and let it cool for an hour. Then place the bowl in the freezer for a few minutes so that the fat settles on the top.
4. Remove the cooked oxtail pieces from the sieve. Put them in a dish and let them cool.
5. Skim the accumulated fat from the top of the cooled soup. Put the liquid in a saucepan and add the prepared chopped vegetables. Bring to a boil, lower the heat, and simmer for 15 minutes. The vegetables should be firm (al dente).
6. Remove the meat from the cooled oxtail pieces, discarding the fat and bones.
7. Taste the soup for seasoning, and add more salt and pepper, if necessary. Add the meat to the soup and heat through. Serve immediately.

Stews

A stew is not a meal one normally associates with single servings. However, as the following recipes show, stews are easily adapted to cooking for one. Try a Brown Gravy Beef Stew, a British Hotpot with Beef and Vegetables, Veal Goulash, or, for variety, a Lamb or Chicken Couscous.

BROWN GRAVY BEEF STEW

½ pound round steak	1 tablespoon vegetable oil
1 tablespoon flour	½ cup beef broth
Salt and freshly ground black	¼ cup chopped onion
pepper	½ bay leaf

1. Pound the meat well with a mallet. Cut the meat into bite-sized pieces.
2. On a piece of wax paper, combine the flour with salt and pepper to taste. Dredge the meat thoroughly.
3. Heat the oil in a heavy pot with a cover. Add the flour-coated beef and brown the beef on all sides.
4. Add the beef broth, onion, and bay leaf to the beef. Stir well. Bring the mixture to a boil, cover, reduce the heat, and simmer for 1 hour. Serve hot.

BOILED BEEF AND VEGETABLES

4 to 6 ounces beef chuck, brisket, or round steak

¼ head of cabbage, cut into thick slices

1 medium-sized onion, peeled and sliced

1 medium-sized carrot, trimmed, washed, and sliced

1 green pepper, cored, seeded, and cut into ¼-inch pieces

2 very small potatoes, peeled, and left whole

⅔ cup beef broth

½ teaspoon dried thyme

½ bay leaf

Salt to taste

Crushed red pepper flakes to taste

Horseradish (optional)

1. Cut the beef into ½-inch pieces and put it into a heavy saucepan with a cover. Add all the other ingredients and mix well.
2. Bring to a boil, cover, lower the heat, and simmer for 1 hour. Serve hot with horseradish, if desired.

BEEF AND TOMATO JUICE STEW

¼ pound beef chuck, cut into cubes

½ cup chopped onion

3 tablespoons dried mushrooms, or several fresh mushrooms, diced

1 5½-ounce can tomato juice

¼ teaspoon dried thyme

Salt and freshly ground black pepper

1. Put all the ingredients in a small heavy pot with a cover.
2. Bring to a boil, cover, reduce the heat, and simmer for 1 to 2 hours, or until the beef is tender. Serve hot, accompanied by mashed potatoes, rice, or any vegetable purée.

FIERY BEEF STEW

Make sure there's plenty of ice water handy when you serve this dish.

1 teaspoon oil	½ small onion, peeled and
4 or 5 ounces beef, cut into	chopped
½-inch cubes	1 stalk celery, trimmed, washed,
½ cut water	and diced
¼ teaspoon chili powder	1 leek, trimmed, halved, washed,
Salt and freshly ground black	and sliced
pepper	1 tablespoon diced hot cherry
½ cup stewed tomatoes	peppers

1. Heat the oil in a small heavy pot with a lid. Add the beef and brown on all sides, stirring frequently.
2. Add the water, chili powder, and salt and pepper to taste. Cover and simmer for 1 hour.
3. Add the stewed tomatoes, onion, celery, leek, and cherry peppers. Simmer for 20 minutes, or until the vegetables are tender. Serve hot.

BEEF IN ALE

1 tablespoon butter	1 cup ale or beer
1 medium-sized onion, peeled	1 bay leaf
and chopped	Pinch of nutmeg
½ pound stewing beef, cut into	Salt and freshly ground black
1-inch cubes	pepper
¼ cup tomato purée	

1. Melt the butter in a suitable skillet. Add the onion and sauté until it is golden.
2. Add the beef to the skillet. Stir and turn the beef to seal all sides of the meat.

3. Transfer the meat and onion to a small heavy pot with a lid. Add the tomato purée and mix well. Add the ale, bay leaf, nutmeg, and salt and pepper to taste. Mix well again.
4. Partly cover and simmer over low heat for 2 to 3 hours. (You should use an asbestos pad so that the meat cooks very slowly.) Cover the pot if the liquid begins to reduce too rapidly. (This dish can also be baked, covered, in a 300-degree oven for 2 to 3 hours.)
5. Taste the sauce, and correct the seasonings, if necessary.

HOTPOT

This was inspired by the Sussex beef dish.

1 medium-sized onion, peeled and thinly sliced	Salt and freshly ground black pepper
½ pound stewing beef, thinly sliced	1 medium-sized potato, peeled and thinly sliced
6 green olives, sliced	1 tablespoon white vinegar
2 stalks celery, trimmed, washed, and chopped	Pinch of ground allspice
1 tablespoon tarragon vinegar	1 whole clove
	3 peppercorns
	¼ cup water

1. Preheat the oven to 350 degrees.
2. Put one half of the sliced onion in the bottom of an ovenproof casserole with a cover. Add half the meat slices, olives, and celery. Sprinkle the tarragon vinegar over all. Season with salt and pepper to taste. Top with one half the sliced potatoes.
3. Make a layer of the remaining onion. Top with the remaining meat slices, olives, and celery. Sprinkle the white vinegar over all. Season with the allspice, clove, peppercorns, and salt and pepper to taste. Top with the remaining sliced potatoes. Pour the water over all.
4. Bake, covered, for 2 hours. An additional tablespoon or so of water may be added in the last half hour to prevent burning.

TWO-REASON BEEF STEW

The reasons: To use tough, leftover beef and to use spinach in beef stew as they do in Japan. This recipe makes a large serving, part of which will taste even better the day after it is made.

4 to 8 ounces tough beef, trimmed of fat and cartilage

1 leek, trimmed, halved, and washed

2 carrots, trimmed, scraped, and washed

1 teaspoon butter

2 medium-sized onions, peeled and chopped

1 ounce fresh spinach, well washed

1 5½-ounce can tomato juice

¼ teaspoon dried thyme

1 bay leaf
Salt and freshly ground black pepper

1 to 2 tablespoons pearl barley, optional

1. Cut the beef into ½-inch dice.
2. Cut the leek and carrots into 1-inch lengths.
3. Melt the butter in a heavy saucepan with a tight-fitting lid. Add the onions and sauté, stirring frequently, until the onions are wilted. Add the beef, onions, leek, carrots, and spinach. Pour the tomato juice over all and mix well. Season with the thyme, bay leaf, and salt and pepper to taste.
4. Bring to a boil, cover, reduce the heat, and simmer for 1 to 2 hours, or until the beef is tender. Add the barley, if desired, during the last hour of cooking.

BRITISH HOTPOT WITH
BEEF AND VEGETABLES

1 medium-sized potato, peeled and sliced
1 medium-sized onion, peeled and sliced
1 stalk celery, trimmed, washed, and chopped

4 to 5 ounces stewing beef, cut into cubes
Salt and freshly ground black pepper
2 tablespoons chopped parsley
1 cup beef broth or water

1. Preheat the oven to 300 degrees.
2. Grease a casserole with a cover. Layer in it one half the potato, onion, celery, and beef. Season with salt and pepper to taste.
3. Layer the remaining onion, celery, beef, and potato, finishing with the potato. Top with parsley. Pour the beef broth over all.
4. Cover the casserole and bake for 3 hours. Remove the cover during the last half hour to allow the top potatoes to brown.

SOUR BEEF

This easy dish is reminiscent of sauerbraten.

½ pound stewing beef, cut into ½-inch cubes
¼ cup white vinegar
1 tablespoon water
2 tablespoons chopped onion
2 tablespoons raisins

Salt and crushed red pepper flakes to taste
2 teaspoons brown sugar
2 whole cloves
2 teaspoons ground allspice

Put all ingredients into a small heavy saucepan with a cover. Bring to a boil over high heat, cover, lower the heat, and simmer for 1 hour. Serve hot with dumplings (see page 161), rice, or potatoes.

BURGUNDY BEEF—1

2 teaspoons vegetable oil
1 slice bacon, cut in quarters
¼ pound beef chuck, cut into ½-inch cubes
1 cup diced carrots
1 medium onion, peeled and chopped
1 clove garlic, peeled and minced
  Salt and freshly ground black pepper
1 tablespoon Cognac
½ cup Burgundy

1. Put the oil into a small heavy pot with a cover. Add one-half of the bacon. Add the cubed beef and top with the carrots, onion, and garlic. Sprinkle with salt and pepper to taste. Put the remaining bacon on top of the meat and vegetables.
2. Pour first the Cognac and then the Burgundy over all. Bring to a boil, cover, turn the heat as low as possible, and cook for about 3 hours. Serve with rice or noodles.

BURGUNDY BEEF—2

¼ to ½ pound beef shoulder or chuck, cut into cubes
2 tablespoons plus 2 teaspoons flour
2 teaspoons olive oil
  Salt and freshly ground black pepper
1 tablespoon Cognac
2 slices bacon or an equal amount of fat ham or fatback, diced
1 clove garlic, peeled and minced
1 carrot, trimmed, scraped, washed, and thinly sliced
2 small onions, peeled and sliced
1 tablespoon chopped parsley
½ bay leaf
½ teaspoon dried thyme
1 cup Burgundy
  Water (optional)
4 teaspoons butter
1 tablespoon lemon juice
5 mushrooms, washed and drained

1. Preheat the oven to 350 degrees.
2. Coat the beef cubes with 2 tablespoons of flour.

3. Heat the oil in a skillet and add the coated beef. Stir and turn the beef cubes until they are brown on all sides. Season the beef with salt and pepper to taste. Pour the warmed Cognac over the beef and ignite it. When the flames die, transfer the beef to a heavy casserole with a cover.

4. Put the diced bacon, garlic, carrot, onions, and ½ tablespoon parsley in the skillet in which the beef was browned. Cook, stirring, until the bacon is crisp. Add the mixture to the beef in the casserole.

5. Add the bay leaf and thyme to the casserole, and pour the Burgundy over all. If necessary, add water to cover the meat and vegetables. Cover the casserole and put it in the oven. Bake for 1 hour.

6. Make a beurre manié by mixing together 2 teaspoons of butter with 2 teaspoons of flour until a paste is formed. Remove the casserole from the oven and add the beurre manié to the liquid a little at a time, until the sauce is slightly thickened. Cover the casserole and return it to the oven for another hour.

7. At the end of the second hour, season the beef with the lemon juice and the remaining parsley. Taste the sauce for salt and pepper, and add more if necessary. Check the beef to see if it is tender. Continued baking if necessary.

8. Slice the mushrooms. Heat the remaining 2 teaspoons of butter in a small skillet. Sauté the mushrooms for about 1 minute and then add them to the casserole, mixing them in.

JUST OXTAILS

1 tablespoon bacon fat or butter	2 carrots, trimmed, scraped, and washed
1 pound oxtail pieces	
Salt and freshly ground black pepper	2 stalks celery, trimmed and washed
1 13¼-ounce can beef broth	4 small white onions, peeled
4 peppercorns	1 teaspoon flour
	2 teaspoons cold water

1. Melt the bacon fat in a heavy pot with a cover. Add the oxtail pieces and brown well on all sides.
2. Add salt and pepper to taste. Add the beef broth and peppercorns. Bring to a boil, cover, lower the heat, and simmer for 3 to 4 hours. Use an asbestos pad and the lowest flame possible.
3. Cut the carrots and celery into thin slices. Add them with the onions to the oxtails. Cover the pot and cook for 1 hour longer.
4. Remove the meat and vegetables from the pot. Strain the sauce through a cheesecloth-lined sieve. Return the sauce to the pot and heat.
5. Mix the flour and water together to make a smooth paste. Add this to the sauce and stir until the sauce thickens. Return the meat and vegetables to the sauce and heat through. Serve with rice, noodles, or boiled potatoes.

OXTAIL RAGOUT

1 tablespoon flour
Salt and freshly ground black
pepper
3 2-inch lengths of oxtail, about
¾ to 1 pound
1 tablespoon vegetable oil
1 bay leaf
½ teaspoon dried thyme
1 stalk celery, washed and
chopped
1 medium-sized onion, peeled
and chopped

1 carrot, trimmed, scraped,
washed, and chopped
1 or 2 cloves garlic, peeled and
crushed
½ cup dry red wine
½ cup beef broth
1 small tomato, peeled, cored,
and coarsely chopped
1 teaspoon flour (optional)
2 teaspoons cold water (optional)

1. Preheat the oven to 350 degrees.
2. On a sheet of wax paper, mix the flour with salt and pepper to taste. Dredge the oxtail pieces in the flour mixture.
3. Heat the vegetable oil in a small heavy skillet. Brown the oxtail pieces well on all sides over medium heat.
4. Arrange the browned oxtail pieces in an ovenproof casserole with a cover. Add the bay leaf, thyme, celery, onion, carrot, garlic, wine, and beef broth. Bring to a boil on top of the stove.
5. Add the chopped tomato, cover the casserole, and bake in the oven for 2 hours, or until the oxtail is tender.
6. Remove the oxtail pieces and keep them warm. Strain the sauce and taste for seasonings, adding more salt and pepper if necessary. If you want a thicker sauce, boil the sauce rapidly to reduce and thicken it. You may also thicken the sauce with a mixture of 1 teaspoon of flour dissolved in 2 teaspoons of water. Serve the ragout hot over noodles or rice.

VEAL DELIGHT

1 teaspoon butter	1 carrot, trimmed, scraped, washed, and sliced
1 small onion, peeled and chopped	¼ teaspoon sugar
1 small tomato, sliced	¼ cup tomato sauce
4 ounces shoulder of veal, cut into 1-inch pieces	Salt to taste
	2 shakes crushed red pepper flakes

1. Melt the butter in a small heavy pot with a cover. Add the onion and sauté the onion until it is translucent.
2. Arrange the tomato slices on top of the onion. Top with the veal. Add the carrot, sugar, tomato sauce, salt, and red pepper.
3. Bring to a boil, cover, lower the heat, and simmer for 2 hours, or until the veal and carrot are tender. Use an asbestos pad and the lowest flame possible. Serve the stew hot.

VEAL AND FRESH PEAS

1 tablespoon butter	1 tablespoon flour
1 scallion, trimmed, washed, and minced	Salt and freshly ground black pepper
4 to 5 ounces stewing veal, cut into 1-inch cubes	½ cup freshly hulled peas
1 teaspoon sugar	½ cup chicken broth

1. Melt the butter in a small heavy pot with a cover. Add the minced scallion. Stir and cook over medium heat until the scallion is wilted, about a minute.
2. Add the veal to the scallions and cook, stirring, until the veal loses its pink color.
3. Sprinkle the veal with the sugar and flour, and mix well. Season with salt and pepper to taste. Add the peas and the chicken broth.
4. Bring to a boil, cover, lower the heat, and simmer for about 15 minutes, or until the peas and veal are cooked. Serve with rice.

VEAL WITH CAULIFLOWER

5 or 6 ounces stewing veal, cut into 1-inch cubes
Water
1 cup chicken broth
3 small white onions, peeled
2 whole cloves
½ bay leaf
Pinch of dried thyme

Salt and freshly ground black pepper
5 cauliflower flowerettes
1 small carrot, trimmed, scraped, washed, and thinly sliced
1 small stalk celery, washed and cut into 1-inch slices
1 egg yolk

1. Put the veal into a small saucepan with a cover and add water just to cover the veal. Bring to a boil and cook for 1 minute. Drain the veal well, but leave it in the saucepan.
2. Add ½ cup chicken broth, 1 peeled onion studded with the cloves, the bay leaf, thyme, and salt and pepper to taste to the veal. Bring to a boil, cover, lower the heat, and simmer for about ½ hour, or until the veal is tender.
3. In another saucepan with a cover, put the cauliflower, the carrot, celery, and the remaining onions and chicken broth. Bring to a boil, cover, lower the heat, and simmer for about 20 minutes, or until the vegetables are tender.
4. Drain the veal and vegetables, retaining the cooking liquids. Keep the veal and vegetables warm in a covered dish. Combine the cooking liquids in a saucepan, and simmer the liquid to reduce it to about ½ cup. Put the egg yolk in a small cup and beat it with a fork. Remove the reduced liquid from the flame. Add a few spoonfuls of the reduced cooking liquid to the beaten egg yolk, and mix it well. Stir the egg into the reduced cooking liquid. Pour the sauce over the veal and vegetables and serve hot. This dish goes very well with rice.

Note: If you are going to prepare the dish in advance, be sure not to boil the sauce or it will curdle.

SPANISH VEAL

¼ pound stewing veal, cut into 1-inch cubes
2 teaspoons flour
Salt and freshly ground black pepper
2 teaspoons olive oil
2 small tomatoes, peeled and diced (about 1 cup)
½ bay leaf

¼ teaspoon dried thyme
¼ teaspoon dried rosemary
2 small white onions, peeled
4 small mushrooms, washed and sliced
3 ripe olives, sliced
1 teaspoon chili powder
1 teaspoon flour (optional)
1 teaspoon butter (optional)

1. Sprinkle the veal cubes with flour and salt and pepper to taste. Turn to coat the veal well.
2. Heat the oil in a skillet and, when hot, add the coated veal cubes. Brown the veal on all sides.
3. Transfer the veal to a small heavy pot with a cover. Add the tomatoes, bay leaf, thyme, rosemary, onions, mushrooms, olives, and chili powder. Bring to a boil, cover, reduce the heat, and simmer for 1 hour. When the veal is tender, you can thicken the sauce by mixing the flour and butter into a paste and stirring it into the sauce.

VEAL GOULASH

¼ pound stewing veal, cut into ½-inch cubes
Salt and freshly ground black pepper
Paprika
1 tablespoon butter or chicken fat
2 teaspoons flour
1 small green pepper, cored, seeded, and cut into 1-inch strips

1 small carrot, trimmed, scraped, washed, and sliced
1 small onion, peeled and chopped
½ teaspoon dried thyme
½ clove garlic, peeled and cut in half
½ cup chicken broth

1. Dust the veal cubes with salt, black pepper, and paprika to taste.
2. Melt the butter in a saucepan with a cover. Add the veal to the pan and brown it on all sides over high heat. This should only take about 1 minute. Stir to keep the veal separated.
3. Sprinkle the veal with the flour and mix well. Cook for another minute or so.
4. Add the remaining ingredients and stir well. Bring to a boil, cover, lower the heat, and simmer for about 20 minutes, or until the veal and vegetables are tender. The vegetables should not be overcooked.

VEAL PAPRIKASH

This is my version of a Belgrade dish. And very tasty it is, too.

¼ pound boneless shoulder of veal, cut into ½-inch cubes
Salt and freshly ground black pepper
1 tablespoon butter
1 small white onion, peeled and diced

1 clove garlic, peeled and cut in half
¼ cup chicken broth
1 teaspoon paprika
2 tablespoons sour cream

1. Sprinkle the veal cubes with salt and pepper to taste. Set aside.
2. Melt the butter in a small heavy pot with a cover. Add the onion and garlic and sauté, stirring frequently, until lightly browned.
3. Add the seasoned veal cubes and cook, stirring, until the veal loses its pink color.
4. Add the chicken broth to the pot and mix well. Bring to a boil, cover, lower the heat, and simmer for 1 hour.
5. At serving time, bring the stew just to a boil and stir in the paprika. Add the sour cream and mix well. Heat the stew, but do not let it boil. Serve with noodles or rice.

VEAL FRICASSEE

¼ pound stewing veal, trimmed and cut into 1-inch cubes
2 teaspoons butter
  Salt and freshly ground black pepper
3 small white onions, peeled and washed
2 cloves
  Pinch of nutmeg
1 clove garlic, peeled and cut into 3 pieces

  Pinch of dried thyme
½ bay leaf
1 teaspoon parsley
¼ cup chicken broth
¼ cup dry white wine
  Pinch of cayenne
2 small carrots, trimmed, scraped, washed, and thinly sliced
¼ cup sliced, washed mushrooms
1 tablespoon lemon juice
1 egg yolk

1. Put the veal cubes in a small bowl. Cover it with cold water and let it stand for an hour. Drain the veal and pat it dry with paper towels.

2. Melt the butter in a small heavy pot with a cover. Add the veal and stir for about 1 minute. Add salt and pepper to taste to the veal. Stick the cloves into one of the onions and add it and the remaining onions to the veal along with the nutmeg, garlic, thyme, bay leaf, and parsley. Mix well and cook for about 1 minute. Add the chicken broth, wine, cayenne, carrots, mushrooms, and lemon juice. Bring to a boil, cover, lower the heat, and simmer for about ½ hour, or until the veal and vegetables are cooked.

3. Using a slotted spoon, remove the veal and vegetables from the sauce and keep them warm. Reduce the sauce to about ¼ cup by boiling it rapidly over high heat.

4. While the sauce is reducing, put the egg yolk into a cup and beat it with a fork. Remove the sauce from the heat and let it cool a little. When it is cool, spoon a little of the sauce into the beaten egg yolk and mix well. Then pour the egg-sauce mixture into the remaining reduced sauce. Heat the sauce over very low heat, stirring constantly. Do not let it boil or it will curdle. Return the veal and vegetables to the sauce to warm. Serve with rice or mashed potatoes.

VEAL WITH SCALLIONS

¼ pound stewing veal, cut into ½-inch cubes	1 tablespoon dry sherry
2 tablespoons vegetable oil	2 teaspoons soy sauce
6 scallions, trimmed and washed	2 teaspoons sugar
1 cup water	Salt to taste

1. Rinse the veal and pat it dry with paper towels.
2. Heat the oil in a skillet with a cover. When the oil is hot, add the scallions and cook, stirring, over high heat until the scallions are brown and crisp, about 5 to 10 minutes. Remove the scallions and set them aside.
3. Add the veal cubes to the same skillet in which the scallions were cooked. Cook the meat over high heat for about 2 minutes, or until the veal begins to brown. Remove the veal and set it aside separately from the scallions.
4. Wipe out the skillet to remove any excess oil. Return the browned veal to the skillet. Add the water, sherry, soy sauce, sugar, and salt to the veal. Bring to a boil and add the scallions. Cover the skillet, lower the heat to very low, and simmer for 1 hour, or until the meat is tender.
5. When the veal is tender, chill it uncovered until the fat rises to the top. Skim off the accumulated fat.
6. When you are ready to serve the dish, reheat the veal and sauce until they are hot. Remove the veal and scallions to a serving dish and keep warm. Reduce the sauce over high heat until it is syrupy and quite reduced. Pour the sauce over the veal and scallions. Serve the dish with rice.

COUSCOUS

2 teaspoons vegetable oil
1 small onion, peeled and chopped
1 clove garlic, peeled and minced
½ pound stewing lamb with bones
1 small leek, trimmed, well washed, and sliced
1 small carrot, trimmed, scraped, washed, and sliced
1 small turnip, peeled and diced

Salt and freshly ground black pepper
Crushed red pepper flakes
1 13 ¾-ounce can chicken broth
½ cup couscous
1 tablespoon butter
1 small zucchini, trimmed, washed, and cut into 1-inch slices
¼ cup canned chick-peas, drained

1. Heat the vegetable oil in a heavy pot with a cover. Add the onion and garlic and sauté until the onion is wilted. Add the lamb, and cook, stirring occasionally, until the meat loses its red color. Add the leek, carrot, turnip, and salt and pepper and crushed red pepper flakes to taste. Stir to mix well. Pour the chicken broth over all. Bring to a boil, partially cover, reduce the heat, and simmer for about 1 hour, or until the lamb is tender.
2. Strain the cooking liquid into another pot with a lid. Cover the stewed lamb and keep it warm. Place a French steamer over the liquid in the second pot. Cover the steamer with cheesecloth. Add the couscous to the steamer. Moisten the couscous with a few drops of water. Cover the couscous and steam it over low heat for 1 hour. Add more water to the bottom of the pot, if necessary.
3. Melt the 1 tablespoon of butter in a small pan. Pour the melted butter over the steamed couscous and mix it in well. Cover the couscous and keep it warm.
4. Pour the liquid from the couscous steamer pot into the reserved lamb and vegetables. Add the zucchini and chick-peas. You may need to add more water. Cover the pot, cook over low heat until the zucchini is tender.
5. Serve a portion of the couscous on a warm plate with the meat and vegetables on top. Moisten to taste with the sauce.

LAMB AND LEEKS

2 medium-sized leeks
½ pound of lamb stew meat and bones
¼ teaspoon thyme

4 small asparagus spears, peeled and cut in 1-inch lengths
1 teaspoon finely chopped mint
1 cup chicken broth
1 tablespoon pearl barley

1. Trim the leeks of roots and all green. Cut in half and wash well under cold running water to remove all sand. Drain well. Slice into ½-inch sections.
2. Place the cut up leeks and all other ingredients into a small heavy pot with a cover. Bring to a boil, cover, turn down the heat, and simmer for 30 minutes.
3. At serving time, bring to a boil again and serve in a hot soup plate.

SIMMERED LAMB AND VEGETABLES

¼ pound boneless lamb, cut into 1-inch cubes
1 medium-sized potato, peeled and sliced
1 large carrot, trimmed, scraped washed, and sliced
1 medium-sized onion, peeled and sliced

¼ teaspoon dried marjoram
½ bay leaf
½ cup beef broth
Salt and freshly ground black pepper
1 teaspoon flour
1 tablespoon water

1. In a small heavy pot with a cover, layer the lamb, potato, carrot, and onion. Sprinkle with the marjoram. Add the bay leaf, beef broth, and salt and pepper to taste.
2. Bring to a boil, cover, lower the heat, and simmer for 1¼ hours, or until the meat is tender.
3. Mix the flour and water together in a tightly covered small jar or in a small cup. Add to the stew and mix it in well. Serve the stew hot.

STOCKHOLDER'S LAMB AND VEGETABLES

This dish can be started before the meeting and then refrigerated to be finished when the meeting is over and you are ready to dine.

10 ounces lamb neck with bones	4 small carrots, trimmed, scraped,
1 cup beef broth	washed, and cut in quarters
½ cup tomato sauce	½ teaspoon dried thyme
2 cloves garlic, peeled and cut in half	Salt and freshly ground black pepper
1 medium-sized onion, peeled and cut in half	1 small potato, peeled and cut in half

1. Put the lamb, broth, tomato sauce, garlic, onion, and 2 of the carrots in a small heavy pot with a cover. Add the thyme and salt and pepper to taste. Bring to a boil, cover, lower the heat, and simmer for 1 hour.
2. Put the covered pot in the refrigerator and go to your meeting.
3. After the meeting, and about 45 minutes before you want to serve dinner, remove the stew from the refrigerator. Skim off and discard the fat that has accumulated on the top of the stew.
4. Add the 2 remaining carrots and the potato to the stew. Bring the stew to a boil, cover, lower the heat, and simmer for about ½ hour, or until the carrots and potato are tender.
5. Using a slotted spoon, remove the meat and vegetables to a hot soup bowl. Add sauce according to your taste and serve hot.

LAST-MINUTE LAMB STEW

This dish is perfect for the evening when your plans change without notice and the lamb is there, but still frozen.

¼ to ½ pound frozen lamb shoulder with bones

1 medium-sized onion, peeled and sliced

1 medium-sized potato, peeled and quartered

2 very large carrots, trimmed, scraped, washed, and sliced 1 inch thick

¼ teaspoon dried thyme

1 bay leaf

1 clove garlic, peeled and sliced

2 tablespoons pearl barley
Water to cover
Salt and freshly ground black pepper
Crushed red pepper flakes

1 teaspoon flour

2 tablespoons water

1. Put the lamb, onion, potato, carrots, thyme, bay leaf, garlic, and barley into heavy saucepan with a cover. Add water to cover the ingredients in the pot. Season with salt, pepper, and crushed red pepper flakes to taste. Bring to a boil, cover, lower the heat, and simmer over very low heat for 1 hour.

2. Using a slotted spoon, remove the meat and vegetables from the saucepan. Cover them and keep them warm. Return the saucepan to the heat and reduce the remaining liquid over medium heat to about ½ cup.

3. Mix the flour and water together in a tightly covered small jar or in a small cup. Add to the reduced liquid and stir well. Taste the sauce for seasonings, adding more salt and pepper, if necessary. Return the reserved meat and vegetables to the sauce and heat through.

PORK WITH POTATOES AND APPLES

¼ pound boneless pork, cut into
   1-inch cubes
1 cup water
½ bay leaf
   Salt and freshly ground black
   pepper

1 medium-sized potato, cut into
   6 pieces
½ small apple, sliced in ¼-inch
   thick slices

1. Put the pork, water, and bay leaf in a small heavy pot with a cover. Add salt and pepper to taste. Bring to a boil, cover, lower the heat and simmer for about 1 hour, or until the pork is tender.
2. Add the potato pieces and simmer for 10 minutes.
3. Add the apple slices and cook for another 20 minutes, or until the apple slices are tender. Taste for seasonings, adding salt and pepper if necessary. Serve hot.

CHICKEN COUSCOUS

1 portion chicken, either breast
   or leg
3 medium-sized carrots, trimmed,
   scraped, washed, and cut into
   1-inch pieces
7 white pearl onions, or an equal
   amount of white onions, peeled
1 stalk celery, trimmed, washed,
   and cut into 1-inch pieces

¼ teaspoon dried thyme
½ bay leaf
½ peeled garlic clove, crushed
½ cup chicken broth
   Salt and freshly ground black
   pepper
½ cup water
¼ cup couscous
1 teaspoon butter

1. Put the chicken in a heavy saucepan with a cover. Add the carrots, onions, celery, thyme, bay leaf, garlic, and chicken broth. Season with salt and pepper to taste. Bring to a boil, cover, lower the heat, and simmer for 1 hour.

2. When the chicken stew has cooked for 40 minutes, bring the ½ cup water to boil in a small pot with a cover. Slowly stir in the couscous. Add the butter and salt to taste. Stir and cook over medium heat for 2 minutes. Cover the pot and let the couscous rest for at least 15 minutes. Keep it warm by placing it over the pilot light of your stove.
3. At serving time, spoon the couscous out on one side of a hot plate, and the chicken stew on the other. Let the sauce mingle with the couscous. Serve immediately.

CHICKEN WITH SAGE DUMPLINGS

1 tablespoon flour	½ cup water
Salt and freshly ground black pepper	1 tablespoon chopped onion
	1 tablespoon chopped parsley
½ chicken breast	Sage dumplings (see recipe
2 teaspoons vegetable oil	page 161)

1. On a sheet of wax paper, mix together the flour and salt and pepper to taste. Use the mixture to coat the chicken on all sides. Reserve any of the flour mixture not used. There should be about 1 teaspoon.
2. Heat the oil in a small skillet. Brown the chicken on all sides. When brown, remove the chicken to a small heavy pot with a cover. Pour off all but 1 teaspoon of the oil from the skillet. Set the skillet aside.
3. Add the water, onion, and parsley to the chicken. Bring to a boil, cover, lower the heat, and simmer for 30 minutes, or until the chicken is tender. Remove the chicken from the broth, set aside and keep warm. Reserve ¼ cup of the cooking liquid. If necessary, add milk to make up this amount.
4. Add the reserved seasoned flour mixture to the skillet in which the chicken was browned. Stir in the reserved cooking liquid. Add the chicken and the spoonfuls of dumpling dough. Cook uncovered for 3 minutes, cover, and cook for an additional 10 minutes. Serve hot.

BRUNSWICK STEW

2 teaspoons bacon drippings or butter
½ chicken breast
½ cup chopped onion
1 medium-sized tomato, peeled, seeded, and cut in large dice
1 clove

¼ teaspoon crushed red pepper flakes
½ cup water
1 ear of corn
½ cup fresh green peas
½ cup cubed green pepper
Salt
¼ teaspoon Worcestershire sauce

1. Heat the drippings in a small heavy skillet. Add the chicken and brown on all sides. Remove the chicken and put it in a saucepan with a cover.
2. Add the onion to the skillet in which the chicken was browned. Sauté the onion until it is brown. Add the onion to the saucepan with the chicken. Add the tomato, clove, crushed red pepper flakes and water to the saucepan. Bring to a boil, cover, lower the heat, and simmer for about 1 hour, or until the chicken is tender. Remove the chicken and let it cool.
3. Cut the corn from the cob and add it to the saucepan with the peas and green pepper. Bring to a boil, cover, reduce the heat, and simmer for about 20 minutes. The vegetables should be crisp, not overcooked.
4. When the chicken is cooled, bone it, and cut it in bite-sized pieces. Add it to the saucepan when the vegetables have cooked. Season the stew with salt to taste and Worcestershire sauce. Mix in well and serve hot.

CHICKEN GUMBO

1 slice bacon	½ cup water
5 ounces boneless chicken	1 tablespoon butter
1 cup chicken broth	½ cup chopped onion
Salt	¼ cup chopped celery
1 ear of corn	¼ cup chopped green pepper
1 medium-sized ripe tomato, peeled, seeded, and diced	2 tablespoons raw rice
⅛ pound okra (about 10 small pods), pared, washed, and sliced	1 teaspoon Worcestershire sauce
	Crushed red pepper flakes

1. In a small frying pan, fry the bacon until it is crisp. Remove the bacon and set it aside for another use.
2. In the same skillet, brown the chicken in the bacon fat. When it is browned, remove it to a small pot with a cover. Pour the chicken broth over the browned chicken, bring to a boil, cover, lower the heat, and cook until the chicken is tender, about 20 minutes. Remove the chicken and let it cool. When cool, cut it into bite-sized pieces. Reserve the chicken broth for step 4.
3. Cut the corn from the cob and put it in a large heavy saucepan with a cover. Add the tomato, okra, and water. Bring to a boil, cover, and set aside.
4. Wipe out the skillet in which the chicken was browned. Add the butter and melt. When the butter is melted, add the onion, celery, and green pepper. Saute over medium heat until the vegetables are wilted, about 2 minutes. Add the sauteed vegetables to the saucepan with the corn, tomatoes, and okra. Stir in the rice and the reserved chicken broth. Season with salt to taste. Bring to a boil, cover, and simmer for about 15 minutes, or until the rice is tender.
5. Add the reserved cubed chicken, the Worcestershire sauce, and crushed red pepper flakes to taste. Mix well and heat until the chicken is hot.

CHICKEN STEW A LA FRANCAISE

½ chicken breast
1 tablespoon lemon juice
2 teaspoons butter
Salt and freshly ground black pepper to taste
2 teaspoons brandy
1 slice bacon
1 tablespoon chopped shallots
2 teaspoons flour
¼ cup chicken broth

¼ cup dry white wine
½ bay leaf
¼ teaspoon dried thyme
3 peppercorns
½ stalk celery, trimmed, washed, and minced
1 medium-sized carrot, trimmed, scraped, washed, and cut in half
1 medium-sized potato, peeled, washed, and cut in half

1. In a small glass bowl, marinate the chicken in the lemon juice for about 20 minutes.
2. In a small skillet, melt the butter. Drain the chicken and pat it dry with paper towels. Sprinkle it with salt and pepper to taste. Brown the chicken on all sides in the melted butter. Remove the chicken and put it into a small ovenproof casserole with a cover. Pour the brandy over the chicken and ignite the brandy. Let it burn out.
3. Wipe out the skillet in which the chicken was browned. Put the bacon in the skillet and cook it until it is very crisp. Remove the bacon and let it drain on a paper towel.
4. Preheat the oven to 375 degrees.
5. Pour most of the bacon grease out of the skillet. Add the shallots and sauté for about a minute. Sprinkle the flour over the shallots and stir to mix well. Add the chicken broth and wine while stirring over medium heat.When the sauce is well blended and begins to thicken, add it to the casserole with the chicken. Add the bay leaf, thyme, peppercorns, celery, carrot, and potato to the casserole. Cover the casserole and bake for 30 minutes, or until the carrot is tender. Crumble the crisp bacon on top. Serve the stew with rice.

Beef

The goodness of a steak or roast depends more on the quality of the raw product than on its preparation. If you choose a good cut of meat, you can be almost certain of an acceptable or even delicious meal. But beef is also the central ingredient in many combination and ethnic dishes. Some of those offered here include London Broil and oxtail recipes, some English dishes such as Shepherd's Pie, and several delicious dishes with a Chinese character, such as Beef and Tomatoes or Beef and Green Peppers.

FILLET MIGNON WITH MINCED TRUFFLES

Salt
¼ pound fillet of beef
Freshly ground black pepper
1 teaspoon butter

1 teaspoon minced truffles
1 teaspoon lemon juice
(optional)

1. Salt the bottom of a small heavy skillet and heat the skillet over a high flame. Add the beef to the skillet and quickly sear it on both sides.
2. Sprinkle the meat with pepper and more salt, if desired. Sauté the beef for 4 minutes to a side for rare, or longer, according to your taste.
3. Remove the fillet to a warm serving plate and keep it warm. Put the butter in the skillet and let it melt, stirring to loosen any brown particles on the bottom of the skillet. Add the minced truffles and cook for 1 minute. Add the lemon juice, if desired. Pour the sauce over the beef and serve immediately.

FILLET OF BEEF WITH MADEIRA SAUCE

¼ to ½ pound fillet of beef
Salt and freshly ground black
pepper
2 teaspoons olive oil
2 teaspoons chopped shallots

1 tablespoon Madeira
2 tablespoons canned beef gravy
or beef broth
1 teaspoon chopped parsley

1. Sprinkle the beef with salt and pepper to taste.
2. Heat the oil in a heavy skillet and sauté the beef. (Three minutes per side should be good for ½-inch thick beef. Five minutes per side should be good for 1-inch thick beef.) Remove the beef to a serving plate and keep it warm.
3. Pour off all but 1 teaspoon of the oil left in the skillet. Add the shallots and stir and cook for 2 minutes. Add the wine and let it cook down and evaporate. Stir in the beef gravy and mix well.
4. Pour the hot sauce over the beef, sprinkle with parsley, and serve immediately.

FILLET OF BEEF WITH VINEGAR GLAZE

1 tablespoon flour
Salt and freshly ground black
pepper
¼ pound fillet of beef, cut into
very thin slices

3 teaspoons butter
1 teaspoon chopped parsley
1 tablespoon red wine vinegar

1. Mix the flour together with salt and pepper to taste on a sheet of wax paper. Coat the beef slices on all sides with this mixture.
2. Heat 2 teaspoons of butter in a heavy skillet. Add the beef and cook for 2 minutes on each side.
3. Transfer the beef to a warm plate and sprinkle it with parsley.
4. Add the remaining butter to the skillet in which the beef was cooked. Heat for a minute, or until the butter begins to brown. Pour the browned butter over the beef slices.
5. Add the vinegar to the skillet and bring it just to the boil. Pour the heated vinegar over the beef and serve the meat hot with rice or potatoes.

CHINESE-STYLE FLANK STEAK

2 teaspoons vegetable oil
¼ pound flank steak, cut into thin strips
1 tablespoon minced onion
½ clove garlic, peeled and minced
4 tablespoons diced celery

2 tablespoons sherry
Salt and freshly ground black pepper
½ teaspoon water
½ teaspoon cornstarch
1 teaspoon soy sauce

1. Heat the oil in a skillet. Add the steak strips and brown them lightly over low heat, stirring constantly.
2. Add the onion, garlic, celery, sherry, and salt and pepper to taste. Mix well and cover. Cook over low heat for 20 minutes.
3. Combine the water, cornstarch, and soy sauce in a small cup. Mix well and stir into the beef. Mix well and heat thoroughly. Serve hot with rice.

PAN-BROILED BEEF WITH SAUCE CHASSEUR

Sauce Chasseur (see recipe page 209)
Salt

¼ pound shoulder or flank steak
1 teaspoon butter
1 teaspoon finely chopped parsley

1. Prepare the Sauce Chasseur and keep it warm.
2. Put salt in the bottom of a heavy frying pan. Heat the frying pan and then add the steak. Cook for 1 minute at high heat, then reduce the heat, and cook for 4 minutes more. Turn the steak and cook for 4 minutes on the second side. This will give you a medium steak; if you prefer a rare steak, cut down on the cooking times.
3. Remove the steak to a warm serving plate. Dot with the butter and sprinkle with the chopped parsley. Serve the Sauce Chasseur on the side.

BEEF STROGANOFF

1 teaspoon paprika Salt and freshly ground black pepper	1 tablespoon plus 1 teaspoon chopped onion
¼ pound fillet of beef, cut into long strips	2 tablespoons dry white wine
1 teaspoon butter	¼ cup sour cream
	2 tablespoons sour pickles (cornichons), cut into thin strips

1. On a sheet of wax paper mix together the paprika and salt and pepper to taste. Coat the beef strips on all sides with this mixture.
2. Melt the butter in a skillet large enough to hold the beef strips in one layer. Add the beef and stir and turn so that the beef cooks evenly. Cook for 2 or 3 minutes. Remove the beef with a slotted spoon, and keep it warm.
3. Add the onion to the skillet and sauté for 1 minute.
4. Turn the heat to low and add the wine to the skillet. Let it cook down until there is only about 1 tablespoon left. Stir in the sour cream and mix well.
5. Return the meat to the skillet and stir to cover the meat with the sauce. Blend in the sour pickles and heat. Serve with rice, mashed potatoes, or noodles.

STUFFED FLANK STEAK

1 recipe for Duxelles (see page 182)	2 teaspoons butter Salt and freshly ground black pepper
¼ pound flank steak	

1. Prepare the duxelles.
2. Lay the flank steak between sheets of wax paper and pound the meat to make it thinner. This will make it easier to stuff.
3. Spoon the duxelles down the center of the pounded flank steak. Roll the steak to enclose the stuffing. Tie the roll with kitchen string in three places around the diameter and once around its length so that the stuffing will not come out during cooking. Alternately, the roll can be closed with toothpicks.

4. Melt the butter in a small skillet with a cover. When the butter is hot, add the meat roll and brown it on all sides. Sprinkle the browned meat with salt and pepper to taste. Cover tightly and cook over very low heat for 1 hour. You may have to use a Flame-Tamer to maintain the lowest heat possible.
5. When the roll is cooked, remove it to a warm plate and snip off the string, or pull out the toothpicks, and serve immediately. Discard any liquid that may have accumulated in the cooking.

MARINATED LONDON BROIL

¼ to ½ pound flank, shoulder, chuck, or top sirloin steak
¼ cup dry red wine
Juice of 1 lemon
1 teaspoon Dijon or Düsseldorf mustard
1 clove garlic, peeled and crushed

¼ teaspoon dried oregano
¼ teaspoon dried chervil
½ teaspoon dried tarragon
1 tablespoon olive oil
Salt and freshly ground black pepper to taste

1. Slice the steak into thin slices so that it will absorb the marinade more easily.
2. Mix all other ingredients in a bowl large enough to hold the beef slices. Add the beef slices and mix thoroughly. Cover and refrigerate for at least 6 hours or overnight. Turn the meat several times during the marinating.
3. When you are ready to cook the meat, remove the slices from the marinade and lay them out in one layer on a broiler pan. Salt the meat lightly again. Preheat the oven and then turn it to broil. Cook 4 to 5 minutes on each side for rare, basting frequently with the remaining marinade; cook the meat longer if you prefer it well done.

POT ROAST WITH CHOCOLATE SAUCE

The chocolate gives this a winy taste reminiscent of Boeuf Bourguignon.

2 teaspoons vegetable oil
¼ pound beef shoulder pot roast
1 small white onion, peeled and thinly sliced
1 small garlic clove, peeled and crushed
1 teaspoon flour
Salt

1 clove
½ bay leaf
¼ cup dry white wine
2 tablespoons water
1 teaspoon red wine vinegar
1 teaspoon grated bitter chocolate

1. Heat the oil in a small heavy pot with a cover. Brown the pot roast well on all sides.
2. Add the onion and garlic to the roast. Stir and cook for 2 minutes, or until the onion is wilted.
3. Add the flour and salt to taste. Stir and blend well.
4. Add the clove, bay leaf, wine, water, and vinegar. Stir well. Bring to a boil, cover, lower the heat, and simmer the roast over low heat for 3 hours.
5. Remove the meat to a warm plate and keep it warm.
6. If there are more than 3 tablespoons of liquid remaining in the pot, reduce the liquid over high heat. Then add the chocolate and stir over medium heat until the sauce is thick and smooth. Pour the sauce over the meat and serve immediately.

POT-ROASTED BEEF WITH MADEIRA-BRANDY SAUCE

Vegetable oil
1 tablespoon flour
Salt
¼ to ½ pound beef shoulder, chuck, or round in one piece

1 small onion, peeled
1 clove garlic, peeled
2 tablespoons brandy
2 tablespoons Madeira

1. Oil the inside of a small heavy pot with a cover.
2. Combine the flour with salt to taste on a sheet of wax paper. Coat the beef well on all sides with the flour mixture.
3. Put the coated beef in the prepared pot and add the onion and garlic. Cover tightly, and cook over medium heat for ½ hour. Then reduce the heat to low and let the roast simmer for 2 hours, or until a good dry coating appears on the bottom of the pot.
4. Remove the beef and onion to a hot plate and keep warm. Discard the garlic.
5. Add the brandy to the pot and stir, over medium heat, to dissolve all of the browned juices. When this is done, add the Madeira and bring to a boil over high heat. Boil rapidly to reduce the sauce by about one-half. Taste for seasonings, and add more salt, if necessary. Strain the sauce over the beef and serve hot.

BEEF TENDERLOIN IN SAUCE CHASSEUR

1 teaspoon butter	1 tablespoon chopped parsley
½ clove garlic, peeled and minced	Salt and freshly ground black
1 teaspoon minced shallots	pepper
1 tablespoon tomato purée	1 teaspoon flour
½ teaspoon dried tarragon	2 tablespoons Madeira Sauce, see
2 tablespoons Burgundy	recipe page 211 (optional)
4 mushrooms, washed and sliced	¼ pound beef tenderloin

1. Melt the butter in a small heavy pot with a cover. Add the garlic and shallots and sauté, stirring, for 1 minute.
2. Add the tomato purée, tarragon, Burgundy, mushrooms, and parsley to the shallots. Season with salt and pepper to taste. Stir and cook for 1 minute.
3. Sprinkle on the flour and mix well. Stir in the Madeira Sauce, if desired. Cover the sauce and remove from the heat. Keep warm.
4. Sprinkle salt in the bottom of a heavy skillet. Heat the skillet and add the tenderloin. Cook for 3 minutes per side for rare, or longer, as desired.
5. Put the beef in the same pot with the sauce. Cover and keep warm until serving time. Reheat, if necessary, at serving time.

JUNIE'S STEAK PIZZAIOLA

1 teaspoon olive oil
6 ounces round or chuck steak
   Salt and freshly ground black
   pepper

1 8-ounce can imported tomatoes,
   drained
1 clove garlic, peeled and cut
   into 3 pieces
½ teaspoon dried oregano

1. Preheat the oven to 375 degrees.
2. Oil the bottom of an ovenproof skillet or baking dish. Sprinkle the steak with salt and pepper and put it in the skillet. Scatter the tomatoes, garlic, and oregano over the beef.
3. Cover the skillet tightly with aluminum foil and bake for 30 minutes. Serve hot.

Note: This dish can also be cooked on top of the stove over very low heat for about 30 minutes, or until the meat is done to your preference.

BRAISED BEEF WITH SEASONED ONIONS

¼ to ½ pound boneless chuck steak
   Salt and freshly ground black
   pepper
1 tablespoon vegetable oil
½ cup chopped onions
½ bay leaf
¼ teaspoon dried thyme

1 whole clove
1 tablespoon red wine vinegar
1 teaspoon prepared mustard
½ cup water
1 tablespoon minced hot cherry
   peppers (optional)

1. Sprinkle the meat on both sides with salt and pepper to taste.
2. Heat the oil in a small heavy pot with a cover. Add the steak and brown for about 4 minutes on each side. Pour off the fat and discard.

3. Add the onions, bay leaf, thyme, clove, vinegar, and mustard to the meat. Stir in the water to blend the seasonings. Add the cherry peppers, if desired.
4. Cover the pot and simmer over very low heat for 2 hours. You may have to use a Flame-Tamer to maintain the low heat. Uncover the pot during the last half hour of cooking to reduce the juices somewhat. Serve hot with unseasoned boiled potatoes.

SWISS STEAK WITH VEGETABLES

1 tablespoon flour	½ cup water
Salt and freshly ground black pepper	¼ teaspoon dried thyme
	½ bay leaf
7 ounces boneless chuck steak, trimmed of excess fat and gristle	1 stalk celery, trimmed, washed, and finely chopped
1 tablespoon vegetable oil	2 teaspoons tomato paste
2 tablespoons chopped onion	3 very small carrots, trimmed, scraped, washed, and diced
½ clove garlic, peeled and minced	½ cup fresh or frozen peas
¼ cup dry white wine	

1. On a sheet of wax paper, mix the flour with salt and pepper to taste. Use this mixture to coat the steak on all sides.
2. Heat the oil in a heavy skillet with a cover. Add the steak and brown it for 5 minutes on each side. Pour the fat out of the skillet and discard it.
3. Add the onion and garlic to the skillet and cook briefly, stirring.
4. Add the wine, water, thyme, bay leaf, and celery. Stir in the tomato paste, cover, and simmer for 1 hour over a very low flame. You may need to use a Flame-Tamer. Add more water, if necessary, to prevent burning.
5. After an hour add the carrots and cook for 20 minutes.
6. Add the peas and cook for 20 minutes, or until the meat and vegetables are tender. Taste for seasoning, and add salt and pepper, if necessary. Serve hot with boiled potatoes or rice.

SWISS STEAK

1   tablespoon flour
¼   teaspoon dry mustard
    Salt and freshly ground black
    pepper
4   or 5 ounces chuck steak, cut
    ½ inch thick

1   teaspoon vegetable oil
1   small onion, peeled and sliced
½   cup canned tomatoes, drained
    and cut up
½   clove garlic, peeled and minced
¼   teaspoon Worcestershire sauce

1. Mix the flour and mustard with salt and pepper to taste.
2. Spread the flour mixture on both sides of the steak and pound
    it in well, using a meat mallet.
3. Heat the oil in a skillet with a cover. Add the steak and brown
    it on both sides.
4. Add the onion, tomatoes, garlic, and Worcestershire sauce.
    Cover and simmer for 2 hours. Serve hot.

CHINESE-STYLE BEEF AND TOMATOES

¼   pound lean beef
2   teaspoons cornstarch
1   tablespoon soy sauce
4   tablespoons vegetable oil
½   cup chopped tomatoes, or an
    equal amount of halved cherry
    tomatoes

½   cup trimmed, washed, and
    sliced scallions
1   scant teaspoon sugar
2   teaspoons dry sherry
2   tablespoons water
    Salt

1. Cut the beef into thin strips about 1½ inches long by ½ inch wide.
2. In a bowl mix together the cornstarch, soy sauce, and 1 table-
    spoon oil. Add the beef strips and mix well. Let marinate for at
    least ½ hour.
3. Heat the remaining 3 tablespoons of oil in a wok or skillet. When
    hot, add the beef strips, and cook over high heat for 1 minute,
    stirring constantly. Remove the cooked beef from the oil using
    a slotted spoon. Set the beef aside.

4. Pour off all but 1 tablespoon of the oil. Return the wok to the heat, and when the oil is hot, add the tomatoes and scallions. Cook for 1 minute, stirring constantly. Stir in the sugar, sherry, and water. Return the reserved beef to the wok, mix well, taste for seasonings, and add salt, if necessary. Serve very hot with rice.

CHINESE BEEF AND GREEN PEPPERS

¼ pound lean beef
1½ teaspoons cornstarch
1½ teaspoons soy sauce
4 tablespoons vegetable oil
1 medium-sized green pepper, cored, washed, seeded, and cut into 2-inch strips

¼ teaspoon sugar
1 teaspoon dry sherry
1 teaspoon water
Salt

1. Slice the beef into thin, narrow strips about 2 inches long.
2. In a bowl mix together the cornstarch, soy sauce, and 1 tablespoon oil. Add the beef strips and mix well. Let marinate for at least 10 minutes.
3. Heat the remaining 3 tablespoons of oil in a wok or skillet. When hot, add the beef strips and cook over high heat for 1 minute, stirring constantly. Remove the cooked beef with a slotted spoon and set it aside.
4. Drain all but 1 tablespoon of the oil from the wok. Return the wok to high heat and add the pepper. Cook, stirring constantly, about 1 minute, or until the pepper is just crisp-tender. Add the sugar, sherry, and water. Stir well. Add the beef and salt, if necessary. Cook, stirring, until just heated through. Serve hot with rice.

STEAK, ONION, AND POTATO PIE

¼ cup flour
2 teaspoons shortening
1 tablespoon cold water
3 teaspoons butter
1 or 2 small potatoes, peeled,
washed, and thinly sliced

1 or 2 small onions, peeled,
washed, and thinly sliced
¼ pound round steak, cut into
small cubes
Salt and freshly ground black
pepper

1. Prepare the crust: Put the flour and a pinch of salt in a small mixing bowl. Work in the shortening, using a pastry blender, a fork, two knives, or a small spatula. The mixture should resemble coarse meal. Add the water and blend until a ball is formed. Refrigerate for ½ hour.
2. Preheat the oven to 350 degrees.
3. Grease a small casserole with 1 teaspoon butter. Make a layer of potatoes on the bottom of the casserole. Top the potatoes with a layer of onions. Salt and pepper the vegetables to taste.
4. Put the meat in a layer on top of the onions. Salt and pepper the meat to taste. Dot the meat with the remaining butter.
5. Roll out the dough on a floured surface or a sheet of wax paper. Shape the dough into a round that will fit the casserole. Put dough on top of the casserole, pressing it against the sides of the casserole. Make a slit in the center of the pastry to allow steam to escape during baking.
6. Bake for 1 hour and serve hot.

SHEPHERD'S PIE

2 small new potatoes
Salted water
2 tablespoons milk
1 teaspoon butter
1 teaspoon oil
1 small onion, peeled and chopped
½ small green pepper, cored, seeded, washed, and chopped

¼ pound ground round or chuck steak
¼ cup cooked sliced carrots
¼ cup cooked green peas
Salt and freshly ground black pepper
1 egg yolk

1. Boil the potatoes in salted water to cover. When they are tender, pour off the water and let them cool until they can be peeled. Mash the potatoes and stir in the milk and butter. Set the potatoes aside.
2. Heat the oil in a small heavy pot. Add the onion and green pepper and sauté, stirring frequently, until the onion is translucent.
3. Add the beef and cook and stir until the meat loses its reddish color. Remove from the heat and stir in the carrots, peas and salt and pepper to taste.
4. Spoon the meat mixture into a small casserole.
5. Add the egg yolk to the mashed potatoes and stir it in well. Top the meat mixture in the casserole with the mashed potatoes and smooth them over with the back of a spoon.
6. Bake the casserole, uncovered, in a 400-degree oven until the meat mixture is bubbling and the potatoes are golden brown. Serve immediately.

GROUND BEEF AND EGGPLANT CASSEROLE

1 small (about 5 ounces) eggplant, peeled	5 ounces ground chuck
1 tablespoon plus 1 teaspoon vegetable oil	⅔ cup chopped tomatoes
½ clove garlic, peeled and minced	1 tablespoon dry rice
1 small onion, peeled and chopped	Salt and freshly ground black pepper

1. Peel the eggplant and cut it into ½-inch-thick slices.
2. Heat 1 tablespoon oil in a large skillet. When hot, add the eggplant slices and brown them lightly on both sides.
3. Remove the eggplant from the skillet and set it aside to drain on paper towels. Add the garlic and onion to the skillet. Stir and add the ground beef. Cook, stirring, until the meat loses its red color.
4. Add the tomatoes, rice, and salt and pepper to taste. Bring just to a boil.
5. Preheat the oven to 350 degrees.
6. With the remaining oil, grease a small casserole with a cover and put half of the eggplant on the bottom. Top the eggplant slices with half the meat mixture. Make another layer of eggplant and top it with the remaining meat mixture. Cover the casserole and bake for 1 hour. Serve hot.

GROUND BEEF AND CHICK-PEA CASSEROLE

1 teaspoon vegetable oil	1 stalk celery, trimmed, washed, and diced
1 small onion, peeled and chopped	1 tablespoon tomato paste
1 clove garlic, peeled and minced	1 teaspoon lemon juice
¼ pound ground round steak	Salt
1 small tomato, washed and diced	Crushed red pepper flakes
1 teaspoon chopped green pepper	¼ cup drained, canned chick-peas

1. Heat the oil in a small heavy pot with a cover. Add the onion and garlic and sauté, stirring, for 1 or 2 minutes, or until the onion is wilted.
2. Add the ground steak and cook, stirring, until the meat loses its red color.
3. Stir in the tomato, green pepper, and celery. Add the tomato paste, lemon juice, and salt and crushed red pepper flakes to taste.
4. Cover and simmer for ½ hour.
5. Stir in the chick-peas and heat through. Serve hot.

GROUND BEEF AND VEGETABLE MEDLEY

1 tablespoon vegetable oil	½ small green pepper, cored, seeded, washed, and cut into ½-inch strips
4 to 5 ounces of ground round steak	
1 tablespoon soy sauce	½ cup drained canned tomatoes
1 medium-sized onion, peeled and thinly sliced	½ teaspoon sugar
	1 teaspoon Worcestershire sauce
1 stalk celery, trimmed, washed, and cut into diagonal ½-inch-thick slices	1 teaspoon Cognac
	1 carrot, trimmed, scraped, washed, and sliced
1 small potato, peeled, washed, and cut into ½-inch cubes	Salt and freshly ground black pepper to taste

1. Heat the oil in a small heavy saucepan with a cover. Add the ground meat and sauté, stirring, until the meat loses its red color. Add the soy sauce and mix well. Cook for 1 more minute.
2. Add the remaining ingredients, mix in well, cover, and simmer for 30 minutes, or until the vegetables are tender. Serve hot with rice.

CHILI WITH BROCCOLI

1 teaspoon vegetable oil
½ cup chopped onion
1 clove garlic, peeled and minced
¼ pound ground chuck or round steak
¼ teaspoon salt
2 teaspoons chili powder
¼ teaspoon crushed red pepper flakes, or to taste
½ teaspoon ground cumin
1 teaspoon dried oregano
½ cup tomato purée or tomatoes passed through a sieve to remove the seeds
2 tablespoons tomato paste
½ cup canned kidney beans with their liquid
1 medium-sized stalk broccoli
Water

1. Heat the oil in a small heavy pot with a cover. Add the onion and garlic and cook, stirring, for 1 minute, or until the onion is wilted.
2. Add the meat and stir to separate it and mix it with the vegetables.
3. Add the salt, chili powder, red pepper flakes, cumin, and oregano. Mix well.
4. Add the tomato purée and tomato paste and simmer, covered, for 1 hour.
5. Put the kidney beans and liquid in a small pot. Begin to heat them when the chili is almost cooked. When they have simmered for a few minutes, add them to the chili.
6. Cut off and discard the main stem of the broccoli, leaving only the broccoli flowerettes. Separate the flowerettes and wash them well. Peel the stems of the flowerettes and slice each flowerette in half. Wash the flowerettes in cool water and drain.
7. Put the cleaned and drained broccoli flowerettes in a saucepan with water to cover. Bring to a boil, lower the heat, and simmer for 5 minutes. Let the broccoli cool a bit in the hot water.
8. Drain the broccoli and put it in a serving bowl. Pour the hot chili over and around it, and serve immediately.

HAMBURGER CASSEROLE

¼ pound ground beef
1 small-sized onion, peeled and chopped
1 medium-sized potato, peeled, washed, and sliced
⅓ cup beef broth

1 teaspoon Worcestershire sauce
1 teaspoon ketchup
Salt and freshly ground black pepper
1 tablespoon grated Cheddar cheese

1. Heat the oven to 350 degrees.
2. In a heavy skillet over medium heat, cook the ground beef, onion, and potato, stirring constantly, until the meat is slightly browned.
3. Transfer the beef mixture to a baking dish and add the broth, Worcestershire sauce, ketchup, and salt and pepper to taste. Mix well.
4. Bake, uncovered, for about 20 minutes, or until the potato is tender.
5. Sprinkle the top with the grated cheese. Put the dish under the broiler until the cheese is melted and bubbly. Serve hot.

APPLE-MEAT LOAF

¼ pound ground round or chuck
2 green onions with tops, trimmed and finely chopped
1 small potato, peeled and grated
1 small onion, peeled and grated
½ small apple, washed and grated

1 small green pepper, cored, seeded, washed, and finely chopped
1 egg
Salt and freshly ground black pepper

1. Preheat the oven to 350 degrees.
2. Mix all ingredients together until they are well blended. If you have a food processor or blender, you can use it for this. In which case, you will not have to grate or chop the vegetables.
3. Line a small ovenproof dish with aluminum foil. Pour the ground meat mixture into the dish. Bake for 1 hour, or until the top of the loaf is dry and crusty.

BEEF-POTATO PATTIES

¼ pound ground round steak	Crushed red pepper flakes
½ cup grated potato	1 tablespoon vegetable oil
1 tablespoon grated onion	1 teaspoon prepared mustard
Salt	1 teaspoon chopped parsley

1. Mix the ground steak, potato, and onion together with salt and red pepper flakes to taste. Form into 4 small patties.
2. Heat the oil and brown the patties on both sides slowly over low heat. This will take about 5 minutes. Remove the patties and keep them warm.
3. Pour off some of the excess oil from the skillet and stir in the mustard and parsley. Combine well and pour the sauce over the patties. Serve immediately.

GROUND BEEF PATTIES WITH COGNAC-CREAM SAUCE

¼ pound ground chuck or round	1 teaspoon finely minced shallots
Salt and freshly ground black pepper	1 teaspoon Cognac
	2 tablespoons light cream
1½ teaspoons butter	1 teaspoon capers (optional)

1. Shape the meat into 2 patties. Sprinkle with salt and pepper to taste.
2. Heat ½ teaspoon butter in a small skillet. Add the patties and cook for 3 minutes to a side for medium. Remove the patties to a warm serving plate and keep them warm.
3. Discard the fat from the skillet and add ½ teaspoon butter. When melted, add the shallots. Cook, stirring, for 1 minute. Add the Cognac and cook for another minute. Add the cream and a dash of salt and pepper. Heat thoroughly and swirl in the remaining ½ teaspoon of butter. Add the capers, if desired, and pour the sauce over the patties. Serve hot.

HAMBURGER WITH SHALLOTS
AND RED WINE

4 or 5 ounces of ground round steak, shaped into a patty	1 tablespoon butter
Salt and freshly ground black pepper	2 teaspoons finely chopped shallots
1 teaspoon vegetable oil	¼ cup dry red wine
	1 tablespoon beef broth or gravy

1. Sprinkle the beef patty with salt and pepper to taste.
2. Heat the oil in a small heavy skillet. Add the beef patty and brown for 3 minutes to a side for rare. Cook longer, if you wish.
3. Transfer the patty to a warm serving plate and keep it warm.
4. Wipe the excess oil from the skillet and add the butter. When it is hot and melted, add the shallots and cook for 1 minute.
5. Add the wine and cook, stirring, until the wine is reduced by half. Add the beef broth and heat through. Pour over the beef patty and serve immediately.

BEEF AND HAM PATTY

4 ounces stewing beef	1 small onion, peeled
3 ounces ham	Salt and freshly ground black pepper to taste
1 stalk celery, trimmed, washed, and cut into 1-inch pieces	

1. Put all ingredients in the container of a food processor or blender. Turn the motor on and off, scraping down the sides of the container, until they are well mixed. If you do not have a food processor, you can grind the beef and ham and dice the celery and onion and mix all together with salt and pepper to taste.
2. Form the mixture into a patty. Heat a heavy skillet and add the patty. Sauté over low heat for 4 to 5 minutes a side to the desired doneness. Serve hot as is, or with your favorite relish or ketchup.

Veal

Good veal at an affordable price is not always easy to find, but it is worth searching for. Veal is joined happily with so many flavors and seasonings that the possibilities for interesting methods of preparation are almost limitless. The recipes suggested in the following chapter range from something as simple as a Sautéed Veal Chop all the way to a more exotic Veal Loaf with Celery Sauce, Calf's Liver in Vinegar, or Veal Sauté Bourguignon.

VEAL WITH TWO VERMOUTHS

1 tablespoon flour	1 tablespoon butter
Salt and freshly ground black pepper	2 tablespoons chopped shallots
	1 tablespoon dry vermouth
6 ounces veal, pounded thin	1 tablespoon sweet vermouth

1. Mix the flour together with salt and pepper to taste. Use this mixture to coat the veal on both sides.
2. In a small frying pan melt the butter over medium heat. Add the veal and cook for 2 minutes on each side.
3. Remove the veal to a warm serving plate and keep it warm. Add the shallots to the frying pan and cook, stirring, for 2 minutes. Pour in both vermouths and stir to dissolve any browned juices in the pan.
4. Cook the sauce until it is reduced to only 1 tablespoon. Then pour it over the veal and serve immediately.

VEAL SCALLOPS WITH MUSTARD

¼ pound thin veal scallops
Salt and freshly ground black
pepper
2 teaspoons Dijon mustard

2 teaspoons butter
Tomato Sauce (see recipe
page 212)

1. Pound the veal lightly with a meat mallet.
2. Sprinkle the veal with salt and pepper to taste.
3. Spread each side of the veal with 1 teaspoon of mustard.
4. Heat the butter in a skillet until it is very hot, but not brown. Add the veal and cook for ½ to 1 minute on each side, depending on the thickness of the veal. Do not overcook. Serve the veal topped with hot Tomato Sauce.

CHINESE-STYLE VEAL AND VEGETABLES

1 medium-sized Italian-style
green pepper
¼ pound veal, thinly sliced
1½ teaspoons cornstarch
2 teaspoons soy sauce
4 tablespoons vegetable oil

1 small onion, peeled and finely
chopped
1 stalk celery, trimmed, washed,
and diced
¼ teaspoon sugar
2 teaspoons sherry
1 teaspoon water

1. Wash, seed, and cut the pepper into small cubes.
2. Cut the veal into 1-inch long strips. Mix the cornstarch, soy sauce, and 1 tablespoon of oil in a bowl. Add the veal and mix well. Let stand for at least 1 hour.
3. Heat the remaining oil in a wok or skillet and cook the veal for 1 minute over high heat, stirring constantly. Remove the veal using a slotted spoon.
4. Discard all but 1 tablespoon of oil in the wok. Heat and cook the green pepper, onion, and celery, stirring constantly, for 1 minute, or until the green pepper is just crisp. Do not overcook. Then add the sugar, sherry, water and salt to taste. (Remember the soy sauce is salty.) Return the veal to the wok and heat through. Serve with rice.

VEAL CHOP WITH CHEESE-BREAD SAUCE

1 veal chop
Salt and freshly ground black pepper
1 teaspoon plus 1 tablespoon butter

1 tablespoon bread crumbs
1 tablespoon grated Parmesan cheese
⅓ cup dry white wine

1. Preheat the oven to 400 degrees.
2. Sprinkle the chop with salt and pepper to taste.
3. Melt 1 teaspoon butter in a skillet and brown the chop on both sides.
4. Mix the remaining butter with the bread crumbs and cheese until it forms a paste.
5. Put the browned chop in an ovenproof dish. Spread the top of the chop with the paste.
6. Bake the chop, uncovered, for 5 minutes. Pour the wine around, not on, the chop and cover it with aluminum foil. Continue to bake for 20 minutes. Serve hot.

SAUTEED VEAL CHOP

½ pound veal chop with bone
Salt and freshly ground black pepper
3 teaspoons butter

1 tablespoon chopped shallots
2 tablespoons dry white wine
¼ cup canned or fresh chicken broth

1. Sprinkle both sides of the chop with salt and pepper to taste. Let the chop rest while preparing the skillet.
2. Put the skillet over medium-high heat and add 2 teaspoons butter. When the butter is melted, tip the skillet and coat the bottom of the skillet completely. When the butter is hot, but not yet brown, add the chop and cook for 1 minute. Turn down the heat and cook the chop for 5 minutes on each side. Remove the chop to a plate and keep it warm in a low oven.

3. Add the chopped shallots to the skillet and cook, stirring, for 1 minute. Add the wine and continue stirring to dissolve any browned juices in the skillet. Let the wine evaporate almost completely. Then add chicken broth. Stir again and cook until there are only about 2 tablespoons remaining. You may have to turn up the heat.
4. Swirl in the remaining butter and pour the finished sauce over the chop. Serve immediately with braised asparagus, celery, or endive.

VEAL CHOP IN VINEGAR SAUCE

¼ pound loin veal chop, trimmed of bone
Salt and freshly ground black pepper
2 teaspoons butter

1 clove garlic, peeled and cut in half
½ bay leaf
¼ teaspoon dried thyme
1 tablespoon wine vinegar
¼ cup chicken broth

1. Sprinkle the veal on both sides with salt and pepper to taste.
2. Heat the butter in a skillet and brown the chop on both sides.
3. Add the garlic, bay leaf, and thyme to the skillet. Stir and cook for 3 minutes.
4. Remove the veal to a small pot with a cover and keep it warm.
5. Pour the vinegar and chicken broth into the skillet. Stir to dissolve any browned juices in the skillet. Pour the sauce over the browned chop, cover, and cook over high heat for 10 minutes. Serve hot.

VEAL SAUTE BOURGUIGNON

¼ pound veal, cut into ½-inch cubes
Salt and freshly ground black pepper
3 teaspoons butter
1 2-ounce can sliced mushrooms, drained
1 tablespoon chopped onion

1 teaspoon chopped shallots
½ bay leaf
½ clove garlic, peeled and minced
Pinch of dried thyme
1 teaspoon flour
1 tablespoon chicken broth
2 tablespoons Burgundy

1. Sprinkle the veal with salt and pepper to taste.
2. Melt 2 teaspoons butter in a skillet. Add the veal and cook over fairly high heat for about 5 minutes, or until one side is quite brown. Turn the meat, reduce the heat, and cook for about 10 minutes. Transfer the meat to a warm serving dish, cover with aluminum foil, and keep warm.
3. Add the mushrooms to the skillet and season them with salt and pepper to taste. Cook for 1 minute. Add the onion, shallots, bay leaf, garlic, and thyme. Stir and cook for 1 minute.
4. Sprinkle the flour over the vegetables. Mix in well. Add the broth and wine. Stir well and cook for 10 minutes.
5. Swirl in the remaining teaspoon of butter. Pour the sauce over the veal and serve immediately.

VEAL AND HAM CASSEROLE

2 tablespoons diced ham fat or bacon
4 or 5 ounces veal shoulder, cut into 1-inch cubes
2 tablespoons diced smoked ham
1 stalk celery, trimmed, washed, and chopped

1 small potato, peeled and diced
1 teaspoon Worcestershire sauce
Salt and freshly ground black pepper
1 tablespoon dry vermouth

1. Preheat the oven to 300 degrees.
2. In a skillet, render the ham fat or bacon of its grease and discard the solids. Add the veal and ham to the skillet and sauté until browned. Transfer the browned meats to a small ovenproof casserole with a cover.
3. Add the celery and potato to the skillet. Cook, stirring constantly, for 2 minutes. Add to the casserole. Season the veal with Worcestershire sauce and salt and pepper to taste.
4. Pour the vermouth into the skillet and stir to dissolve any browned juices in the skillet. Add the vermouth to the veal.
5. Cover the casserole and bake for 1½ hours. Serve hot.

VEAL-VEGETABLE CASSEROLE

1 teaspoon butter	1 teaspoon water
1 tablespoon chopped onion	Pinch of paprika
5 ounces veal shoulder, cut into 1-inch cubes	½ bay leaf
	Salt and freshly ground black
1 tablespoon tomato sauce	pepper
3 tablespoons beef or chicken broth or water	1 small potato, peeled, quartered, and cooked
1 teaspoon flour	¼ cup cooked and drained peas

1. Preheat the oven to 350 degrees.
2. Melt the butter in a skillet. Add the onion and sauté until it is translucent. Add the veal and saute until it is brown on all sides. Transfer the onions and veal to a small ovenproof casserole with a cover.
3. Pour the tomato sauce and broth into the skillet. Bring to a boil and cook for 2 minutes.
4. Blend the flour and water in a cup and stir into the sauce. Season the sauce with paprika, bay leaf, and salt and pepper to taste.
5. Pour the sauce over the veal in the casserole. Cover and bake for 1 hour.
6. Arrange the cooked potato and peas around the veal. Cover and cook for 5 minutes. Serve hot.

VEAL CHILI

1 ear of corn
1 tablespoon flour
   Salt and freshly ground black
   pepper
¼ pound veal shoulder, cut into
   ½-inch cubes
2 teaspoons vegetable oil
2 teaspoons chili powder
1 clove garlic, peeled and minced

½ teaspoon ground cumin
¼ teaspoon dried oregano
⅓ cup beef broth
1 small green pepper, cored,
   seeded, washed, and diced
1 tablespoon butter
2 olives, cut in half
1 tablespoon chopped pimiento

1. Cut the corn off the cob and set aside.
2. Mix the flour with salt and pepper to taste. Dredge the veal with the mixture.
3. Heat the oil in a small pot with a cover. Add the veal and brown on all sides.
4. Add the chili powder, garlic, cumin, and oregano. Stir well and add the broth. Stir to dissolve any browned juices clinging to the pan. Cover and simmer for ½ hour.
5. Melt the butter in a skillet. Add the pepper and cook until it is just crisp. Add the corn and cook, stirring, for 2 minutes. Add to the veal.
6. Add the olives and pimiento to the veal. Blend well, and serve with rice.

VEAL CURRY

1 tablespoon plus 2 teaspoons
   butter
1 clove garlic, peeled and minced
1 tablespoon minced onion
1 tablespoon finely chopped apple
1 tablespoon finely chopped
   banana
½ tablespoon tomato sauce

⅓ cup chicken broth
1 teaspoon flour
4 ounces veal, cut into ½-inch
   cubes
   Salt and freshly ground black
   pepper
2 tablespoons light cream

1. Melt 1 tablespoon butter in a small saucepan with a cover. Add the garlic and sauté for ½ minute. Then add the onion and sauté until just soft. Stir so that the vegetables do not brown.
2. Add the apple, banana, and tomato sauce and cook, stirring, for 1 minute. Stir in the chicken broth.
3. Mix 1 teaspoon butter and the flour together to form a paste. Add the paste, little by little, to the sauce, stirring constantly. Cover the saucepan and set it aside in a warm place.
4. Sprinkle the veal lightly with salt and pepper.
5. Melt the remaining teaspoon butter in a skillet. When hot, add the veal and cook, stirring, for 2 minutes.
6. Using a slotted spoon, transfer the veal to the saucepan. Add the cream and stir in well. Serve hot.

VEAL AND EGGPLANT CASSEROLE

1 tablespoon flour	1 small eggplant, peeled and
Salt and freshly ground black	chopped
pepper	1 tomato, peeled and chopped
¼ pound veal, cut into ½-inch	2 tablespoons chopped green
cubes	pepper
2 teaspoons vegetable oil	1 stalk celery, trimmed, washed,
1 clove garlic, peeled and	and chopped
crushed	¼ cup chicken broth
1 very small onion, peeled and	1 tablespoon raw rice (optional)
chopped	

1. Mix the flour together with salt and pepper to taste. Use this mixture to dredge the veal on all sides.
2. Heat the oil in a saucepan with a cover. Add the veal and brown on all sides. Stir in the garlic and onion, and cook for 2 minutes more.
3. Add the remaining ingredients, except the rice. Bring to a boil, lower the heat, cover, and simmer for 1 hour.
4. Add the rice for the last 20 minutes, if desired. Serve hot.

BRAISED VEAL SHANK

1 small veal shank	¼ cup plus 2 teaspoons dry white
Salt and freshly ground black	wine
pepper	¼ cup chicken broth
1 tablespoon butter	¼ cup chopped tomatoes
½ cup sliced onion	2 sprigs fresh parsley
¼ cup diced celery	½ bay leaf
¼ cup sliced carrot	¼ teaspoon dried thyme
1 clove garlic, peeled and	1 teaspoon cornstarch
quartered	½ cup drained canned peas
	(optional)

1. Sprinkle the veal shank with salt and pepper to taste.
2. Melt the butter in a heavy pot with a cover. Add the shank and brown slowly on all sides. When the shank is browned, add the onion, celery, carrot, and garlic to the veal. Cook over low heat for a few minutes. Then add ¼ cup dry white wine, the chicken broth, tomatoes, parsley, bay leaf, thyme, and salt and pepper to taste.
3. Cover the pot and cook over low heat for about 2 hours, or until the meat is fork tender. Remove the veal and keep it warm.
4. Strain the sauce through a fine sieve, pushing as much liquid as possible out of the cooked vegetables.
5. Mix together the cornstarch and remaining 2 teaspoons of wine.
6. Return the strained sauce to the pot. Bring to a simmer and blend in the mixed cornstarch and wine. Cook until the sauce thickens. Return the veal shank to the sauce, and add the peas, if desired. Heat through and serve with noodles or rice.

VEAL LOAF WITH CELERY SAUCE

4   to 6 ounces ground veal
1   slice white bread, trimmed
    and crumbled
1   small onion, peeled and
    chopped
1   very small carrot, trimmed,
    scraped, washed, and chopped
1   egg
½   teaspoon plus a pinch dried
    thyme

Salt
Crushed red pepper flakes
Oil
1   slice bacon, cut in 3 pieces
2   stalks celery, trimmed, washed,
    and finely chopped
½   cup chicken broth
1   teaspoon flour
2   teaspoons water

1. Preheat the oven to 350 degrees.
2. Mix the veal with the crumbled bread, onion, carrot, and egg.
   Season with thyme and salt and crushed red pepper to taste.
3. Line a small baking pan with aluminum foil and oil the foil on
   the bottom of the pan.
4. Mold the meat mixture into a round or oval loaf and put the
   loaf on the oiled foil. Top the loaf with the bacon pieces and
   bake for 1 hour.
5. Prepare the sauce: Put the celery and broth in a small saucepan
   with a cover. Season with a pinch of thyme and salt to taste.
   Cover and simmer until well done. Stir the flour and water together in a cup and stir into the sauce to thicken it. Keep warm
   until the veal loaf is cooked.
6. Serve the loaf warm or hot with the celery sauce.

Note: This loaf is also good with Tomato Sauce, Mushroom
Sauce, or ketchup. It is also good plain.

VEAL PATTY IN LEMON SAUCE

¼ pound veal, cut into cubes
1 egg yolk
1 slice white bread, trimmed of crust and diced
1 small onion, peeled and sliced
Salt and freshly ground black pepper

2 teaspoons butter
1 teaspoon chopped shallot
2 teaspoons flour
2 tablespoons dry white wine
¼ cup chicken broth
1 tablespoon lemon juice
1 teaspoon sugar

1. Put the veal, egg yolk, white bread, and onion in the container of a food processor or blender. Add salt and pepper to taste. Turn the motor on and off until the ingredients are uniformly chopped. (In the absence of a food processor or blender, grind the veal and mince the onion, and blend them together with the egg and bread.)
2. Form the meat mixture into a patty and refrigerate it for ½ hour or more.
3. Melt the butter in a small saucepan with a cover. Add the shallot and sauté for 1 minute. Sprinkle the flour over the shallot and stir and cook for 1 minute. Add the dry white wine and stir again. Mix in the chicken broth and cook for 1 minute, stirring. Blend in the lemon juice and sugar.
4. Add the patty to the sauce. Cover the saucepan and cook over low heat for 20 minutes. The sauce should simmer, not boil. Serve with rice, potatoes, or noodles.

MOCK VEAL HASH DELMONICO

1 tablespoon oil
3 or 4 ounces diced veal
½ small onion, peeled and minced
1 small potato, peeled and diced
2 tablespoons chopped pimiento
1 egg yolk

¼ cup half and half
4 stuffed olives, drained and sliced
1 hard-boiled egg, finely chopped
Salt and freshly ground black pepper

1. Heat the oil in a small heavy pot with a cover. Add the diced veal and the onion. Stir and cook for 1 minute.
2. Add the potato and pimiento and stir. Cover and simmer for 12 minutes, or until the potato is just tender.
3. Mix together the egg yolk and half and half and add to the veal with the chopped olives and diced egg. Season with salt and pepper to taste. Serve over toast or with rice or corn bread.

POACHED VEAL LOAF WITH CAPERS

¼ pound veal
1 small onion, peeled and sliced
1 slice trimmed white bread, crumbled
1 egg yolk
2 stalks celery, trimmed, washed, and cut into 1-inch pieces

Salt
Crushed red pepper flakes
2 teaspoons butter
2 teaspoons flour
2 tablespoons dry white wine
½ cup chicken broth
1 tablespoon drained capers

1. Put the veal, onion, white bread, egg yolk, and celery in the container of a food processor or blender. Add salt and red pepper flakes to taste. Turn the motor on and off until the ingredients are uniformly chopped. (In the absence of a food processor or blender, grind the veal and mince the onion and celery, and blend them together with the bread crumbs and egg yolk.) Form the meat mixture into a loaf and refrigerate for at least ½ hour.
2. Melt the butter in a small saucepan with a cover and blend in the flour. Cook for a few seconds and add the wine. Stir to smooth out any lumps. Add the chicken broth and continue to stir. When well blended, add the veal loaf to the sauce. Cover and simmer for 1 hour. Just before serving add the capers to the sauce.

BAKED CALF'S LIVER

1 tablespoon flour	1 teaspoon vegetable oil
Salt and freshly ground black pepper	1 small onion, peeled and thinly sliced
7 ounces calf's liver	2 slices bacon

1. Preheat the oven to 350 degrees.
2. Mix the flour with salt and pepper to taste. Use this mixture to coat both sides of the liver.
3. Pour the oil into a roasting pan just big enough to hold the liver. Spread the oil around the pan and add the coated liver. Top the liver with the onion slices and the bacon. Bake for 30 minutes and serve immediately.

CALF'S LIVER IN VINEGAR

2 tablespoons flour	2 tablespoons butter
Salt and freshly ground black pepper	½ tablespoon parsley
4 or 5 ounces calf's liver, thinly sliced	1 tablespoon red wine vinegar

1. Mix the flour together with salt and pepper to taste. Use this mixture to dredge the liver on both sides.
2. Melt 1 tablespoon butter in a small skillet. Add the liver and sauté, over medium heat, for 3 minutes on each side. Do not overcook.
3. Transfer the cooked liver to a heated plate and sprinkle it with parsley.
4. Add the remaining butter to the skillet, swirl it around, and cook it for 1 minute. Pour the melted butter over the liver.
5. Put the vinegar into the skillet and bring it to a boil. Pour the hot vinegar over the liver and serve immediately.

Lamb

Although a roast leg of lamb makes a tasty and enjoyable meal, dishes less in quantity than a roast are more suited to the individual life-style. This flavorful meat offers itself to such diverse dishes as Pan-broiled Loin Lamb Chops, Shoulder Lamb Chops with Dill, Lamb-stuffed Eggplant, and even a delicious Lamb Curry.

BROILED RACK OF LAMB

½ rack of lamb or 3 or 4 rib lamb chops
Salt and freshly ground black pepper

1 tablespoon olive oil
1 tablespoon butter
2 teaspoons chopped parsley

1. Cut away and discard most of the fat leaving only a thin layer of top fat. French the bone ends by cutting away all fat and tissue from 1 inch or so of the chops or ribs and leaving the bare bone ends to be decorated with paper frills (optional).
2. Preheat the broiler to hot.
3. Salt and pepper the lamb to taste on both sides and sprinkle all over with olive oil.
4. Place the lamb fat side down on a rack in the broiler and cook for 5 minutes.
5. Turn the lamb and broil for 5 minutes on the other side.
6. Turn off the oven and open the door. Let the lamb rest several minutes before serving well buttered and sprinkled with parsley.

PAN-BROILED LOIN LAMB CHOPS

2 loin lamb chops
¼ teaspoon oregano
¼ teaspoon minced garlic

Salt and freshly ground black pepper
1 teaspoon chopped parsley
1 teaspoon butter

1. Wipe the meat with a paper towel and trim off most of the fat and discard it. Sprinkle the meat on both sides with the oregano, garlic, and salt and pepper to taste. Press the spices into the meat.
2. Heat a small frying pan over moderate heat and sprinkle the bottom with salt.
3. Place the chops in the heated pan and shuffle them around to prevent sticking and burning. Cook for 3 to 6 minutes on each side, according to your taste and the thickness of the chops. Chops 1½ inches thick will be tender and rare at 3 minutes per side, using moderate heat.
4. Remove the chops to a warm plate and top with the butter.

BAKED SHOULDER LAMB CHOP

1 teaspoon vegetable oil
1 6-ounce shoulder lamb chop, including bone
Salt and freshly ground black pepper
1 small tomato, cored, washed, and sliced

1 small onion, peeled and thinly sliced
½ teaspoon dried oregano
1 teaspoon chopped parsley
2 tablespoons water

1. Preheat the oven to 400 degrees.
2. Oil a small casserole with a cover and add the chop. Move it around to coat the chop evenly with the oil.
3. Sprinkle the chop with salt and pepper to taste and cover it with the tomato slices and then the onion slices. Season again with salt and pepper and sprinkle the oregano and parsley over all.
4. Add the water and cover the casserole. Bake, covered, for 50 minutes. Uncover and turn the chop. Bake for another 10 minutes. Serve hot with rice or boiled potatoes.

SWEDISH-STYLE ROAST LAMB

This recipe was inspired by Liz Kinne's Swedish-style leg of lamb.

1 large shoulder lamb chop	1 teaspoon sugar
Salt and freshly ground black	1 teaspoon flour
pepper	¼ cup milk
¼ cup black coffee	1 teaspoon currant jelly
1 teaspoon light cream	

1. Preheat the oven to 350 degrees.
2. Wipe the lamb chop with a paper towel and rub both sides with salt and pepper to taste.
3. Put the lamb on a rack in a roasting pan and roast uncovered for 1 hour.
4. Combine the coffee, cream, and sugar.
5. Remove the lamb and rack from the roasting pan and discard the excess fat in the pan. Return the lamb to the pan and pour the coffee mixture over all. Roast, uncovered, for ½ hour, turning the lamb once or twice. Transfer the lamb to a warm plate.
6. Add the flour to 2 tablespoons of the sauce (discarding any excess sauce) and stir and cook for a few seconds. Add the milk and stir constantly until thickened.
7. Remove the pan from the heat and stir in the currant jelly. Mix well and serve the sauce over the lamb.

SHOULDER LAMB CHOP WITH DILL

1 teaspoon vegetable oil	Salt and freshly ground black
1 7-ounce shoulder lamb chop,	pepper
including bone	2 tablespoons chopped fresh dill

1. Heat the oil in a small skillet with a cover. Add the chop and brown on both sides.
2. Season the chop with salt and pepper to taste and sprinkle it with the dill. Cover and simmer for 1 hour. Serve hot.

SKEWERED LAMB

¼ pound boneless lean lamb, cut
into 1-inch cubes
Salt and freshly ground black
pepper
2 teaspoons olive oil

6 small mushrooms
4 1-inch squares of green pepper
1 medium-sized white onion,
peeled and cut into 4 slices
4 cherry tomatoes

1. Put the lamb cubes in a small bowl and season them with salt and pepper to taste. Add the olive oil and let the lamb marinate for at least ½ hour, turning it several times.
2. Preheat the oven to 400 degrees.
3. Put the lamb on 8-inch skewers, arranging it in this order: mushroom, green pepper, lamb, onion, tomato, and mushroom.
4. Put the skewers on a rack in a roasting pan and bake for 15 minutes. Turn the skewers and bake for another 15 minutes.
5. Holding the handle end of each skewer with a pot holder, push the food off the skewers onto a warm plate with a fork.

LAMB CURRY

2 teaspoons vegetable oil
4 or 5 ounces lean boneless
shoulder of lamb, cut into
1-inch cubes
¼ cup thinly sliced carrots
1 stalk celery, trimmed, washed,
and coarsely chopped
½ cup coarsely chopped onion
½ cup coarsely chopped tart
green apple

½ clove garlic, peeled and crushed
½ bay leaf
⅛ teaspoon dried thyme
1 tablespoon curry powder
2 teaspoons flour
¼ cup canned tomatoes
½ cup chicken broth
1 tablespoon chutney
2 teaspoons heavy cream

1. Preheat the oven to 400 degrees.
2. Heat the oil in a heavy skillet. Add the lamb and brown well on all sides. When the cubes are browned, transfer them to a flame-proof casserole with a cover.
3. Add the carrots, celery, and onion to the skillet and sauté over low heat for 5 minutes. Add to the meat in the casserole.
4. Add all the other ingredients, except the heavy cream, to the casserole and mix well. Bring to a boil on top of the stove. Cover and put in the oven. Bake for 1 hour.
5. Remove the casserole from the oven and transfer the lamb to a plate. Cover and keep it warm.
6. Purée the sauce and return it to the casserole with the meat. Stir in the cream and bring the sauce just to a boil. Serve with rice and additional chutney.

LAMB-STUFFED EGGPLANT

1 small eggplant, trimmed and washed	1 small onion, peeled and chopped
Salt and freshly ground black pepper	6 ounces ground lamb
	¼ cup tomato sauce
1 teaspoon olive oil	2 tablespoons beef broth
	1 teaspoon lemon juice (optional)

1. Cut the eggplant in half lengthwise. Scoop out and discard some of the center flesh, being sure to leave a good cavity for the stuffing. Sprinkle the eggplant cavities with salt and let them rest for at least 15 minutes. Rinse well and dry with paper towels.
2. Preheat the oven to 350 degrees.
3. Heat the oil in a small skillet and sauté the onion for 1 minute. Add the meat. Cook, stirring occasionally, until the meat loses its reddish color. Season with salt and pepper to taste.
4. Put the eggplant halves in an ovenproof casserole and stuff each with the meat mixture. Combine the tomato sauce and broth with the lemon juice, if desired, in a small saucepan. Simmer for a few minutes. Pour the sauce over and around the eggplant.
5. Bake, uncovered, for 30 minutes, or until the eggplant flesh is fork-tender. Serve hot with the sauce.

LAMB SHANK WITH HERBS

1 ¼- to ½-pound lamb shank
¼ cup tomato purée
¼ cup dry white wine
1 medium-sized onion, peeled and thinly sliced
1 tablespoon brown sugar

1 clove garlic, peeled and crushed
1 teaspoon dried dill
¼ teaspoon oregano
¼ teaspoon rosemary
   Salt and freshly ground black pepper

1. Preheat the oven to 300 degrees.
2. Put the lamb shank in a casserole or baking dish with a cover.
3. Mix the other ingredients together and add them to the lamb.
4. Cover the casserole and bake for 3 hours.
5. Uncover the casserole and bake for another ½ hour. Serve hot with rice and sauce, as desired. You may boil the sauce down to reduce it if it is too thin.

BRAISED LAMB SHANK

1 1-pound lamb shank
   Salt and freshly ground black pepper
1 small onion, peeled and thinly sliced
1 clove garlic, peeled and minced
½ teaspoon dried, crushed oregano
1 small green pepper, cut into 1-inch cubes

⅓ cup diced tomatoes
1 small eggplant, trimmed, washed, and cut into 1-inch cubes
1 small zucchini, trimmed, washed, and cut into 1-inch cubes

1. Preheat the oven to 400 degrees.
2. Sprinkle the lamb shank with salt and pepper to taste and put it in an open baking dish. Bake for 30 minutes.
3. Turn the lamb and bake it for another 15 minutes.
4. Scatter the remaining ingredients around the lamb. Add salt and pepper to taste, and continue baking for another 30 minutes.
5. Test the lamb. It should be fork-tender. If it is not, reduce the heat to 300 degrees and cook for another 15 minutes. Serve with rice or noodles.

LAMB LOAF

Oil

4 or 5 ounces ground shoulder of lamb

1 slice white bread, trimmed and crumbled

2 tablespoons milk

1 egg

4 tablespoons chopped celery

Salt and freshly ground black pepper

1. Preheat the oven to 350 degrees.
2. Oil a small casserole with a cover.
3. Mix all ingredients thoroughly and put them into the casserole.
4. Bake, covered, for 1 hour. Uncover and brown the top. Serve hot, plain, or with relish, ketchup, or horseradish.

PAN-BROILED LAMB PATTIES

3 teaspoons butter

1 tablespoon chopped onion

¼ pound ground lean lamb

2 tablespoons bread crumbs

1 tablespoon finely chopped dill

1 egg yolk

Salt and freshly ground black pepper

2 tablespoons sliced mushrooms

1 teaspoon chopped shallots

1 tablespoon dry white wine

2 tablespoons cream

1. Melt 1 teaspoon butter in a small skillet. Add the onion and cook until wilted.
2. Combine the meat with the sautéed onion, bread crumbs, dill, egg yolk, and salt and pepper to taste. Shape into 2 patties.
3. Heat 1 teaspoon of butter in a skillet and cook the patties for 3 or 4 minutes on each side. Remove the patties and keep warm. Wipe out the skillet.
4. Heat the remaining butter and cook the mushrooms until they are lightly browned. Add the shallots and wine and cook until the wine is almost evaporated. Add the cream and cook for 1 minute. Pour the sauce over the patties and serve immediately.

Pork

Good pork is readily available in city markets today, and I use it frequently. The flavor of a moist, well-cooked cut of pork, whether it's Roast Pork with Apple Sauce, Stuffed Pork Chops, or a Pork Chop, Sauerkraut, and Apple Casserole is hard to beat. In several recipes such as Ham and Asparagus in Cheese Sauce or Apple-topped Country Ham Steak, I recommend the use of country-cured ham for added flavor, however, any good cut of ham will make a flavorful and delicious meal.

ROAST PORK WITH SAUERKRAUT

1 small onion, peeled and sliced
½ tart apple, cored, peeled and sliced
2 small potatoes, peeled and washed

Salt and freshly ground black pepper
1 8-ounce can sauerkraut, drained
7 to 9 ounces boneless pork roast with fat

1. In a small heavy pot with a cover, layer the onion, apple, and whole potatoes, sprinkling each layer with salt and pepper. Top with the sauerkraut and set aside.
2. Cut the pork as necessary to remove as much fat as possible. Irregular pieces are acceptable.
3. Put the pork and the fat into a skillet. Render as much fat as possible while the pork browns for 15 minutes.
4. Add the browned pork to the vegetables. Sprinkle it with salt and pepper. Cover the pot, put it on a Flame-Tamer, and cook for 2 hours, or until the pork is tender. Serve hot.

ROAST PORK WITH APRICOTS

½ pound boneless pork roast
Salt and freshly ground black
pepper to taste

½ cup apricot halves with juice
1 teaspoon cornstarch
2 teaspoons water

1. Preheat the oven to 350 degrees.
2. Season the pork with salt and pepper to taste and put it on a rack in a shallow roasting pan.
3. Roast the pork for 1 hour and discard the liquid fat.
4. Place the pork in a small flame-proof casserole with cover.
5. Separate the apricot halves and liquid. Pour the apricot liquid over the pork, cover the casserole and bake for ½ hour. Remove the pork to a warm plate.
6. Mix the cornstarch and water in a cup and stir this mixture into the liquid remaining in the casserole. Bring to a boil and cook for 1 minute.
7. Place the apricot halves on and around the pork on the serving plate and spoon several tablespoons of the sauce from the casserole over all. Serve hot.

ROAST PORK WITH APPLE SAUCE

¼ pound boneless pork roast
Salt and freshly ground black
pepper

4 ounces apple sauce

1. Preheat the oven to 350 degrees.
2. Sprinkle the pork with salt and pepper to taste. Put the roast on a rack in a shallow roasting pan.
3. Roast the pork in the preheated oven for 1 hour. Discard the liquid fat and transfer the pork to a small casserole with a cover.
4. Spoon the apple sauce over the pork, cover and return the pork to the oven. Cook for 1 hour more and serve hot.

PORK PAPRIKASH

¼ pound boneless pork loin
Salt and freshly ground black
pepper to taste
½ teaspoon paprika
2 teaspoons butter

1 tablespoon chopped shallots
or onion
2 tablespoons dry white wine
2 tablespoons chicken broth
2 tablespoons sour cream
Chopped parsley

1. Trim the pork of fat. Pound the pork lightly between sheets of wax paper.
2. Salt and pepper the pork on both sides and sprinkle both sides liberally with paprika.
3. Melt the butter in a skillet and cook the pork over high heat for 3 minutes on each side. Remove the meat to a warm serving plate and keep it warm in the oven.
4. Pour off any excess fat in the skillet and add the chopped shallots. Stir and cook over low heat for 1 minute, or until they are wilted.
5. Pour the wine into the skillet and stir to dissolve any browned juices. Let the wine half evaporate and add the chicken broth. Mix well and cook, stirring, for about 1 minute.
6. Take the skillet off the flame and swirl in the sour cream.
7. Remove the pork and its warm plate from the oven and pour sauce over the pork. Garnish with parsley. Serve immediately.

BRAISED PORK AND TURNIPS

1 teaspoon vegetable oil	Salt to taste
5 ounces boneless pork	2 small turnips or about a cup of
½ teaspoon dried thyme	peeled and sliced turnips

1. Heat the oil in a small heavy pot with a cover. Add the pork and brown well on both sides.
2. Sprinkle the pork with the thyme and salt to taste. Place the slices of turnip on top of the pork and cover the pot.
3. Put the casserole over a Flame-Tamer and cook at low heat for about 1 hour, or until the turnips are done.

BREADED PORK CHOP

1 egg	1 pork chop, trimmed of fat and
Salt and freshly ground black	bone, if desired
pepper	1 teaspoon butter
1 slice white bread, trimmed and	
crumbled by hand or in a	
blender	

1. Break the egg into a saucer and season it with salt and pepper to taste. Beat until well blended.
2. Dip both sides of the pork chop into the bread crumbs and then into the egg. Dip again into the crumbs and then into the egg. Press the crumbs into the meat to help them adhere.
3. Melt the butter in a small skillet with a cover. When it is hot, add the chop and brown on both sides. Cover the skillet and cook the chop for about ½ hour, turning, or until it is well done. Serve hot.

STUFFED PORK CHOPS

2 medium or 1 large pork chop
1 tablespoon butter
1 tablespoon finely chopped onion
2 tablespoons dried mushrooms or slightly more fresh mushrooms

1 tablespoon chopped or crumbled Roquefort cheese
2 tablespoons bread crumbs
Salt and freshly ground black pepper

1. Preheat the oven to 325 degrees.
2. Trim most of the fat from around the edges of the chops with a sharp knife. Carefully make a pocket in each chop by inserting the knife in the side away from the bone and cutting toward the bone. Make the pocket as large as possible without cutting through the meat at the sides.
3. Melt the butter in a skillet and sauté the chopped onion and mushrooms for about 4 minutes, stirring constantly. Remove the skillet from the heat and stir in the cheese and bread crumbs. Blend well.
4. Stuff the chops with this mixture, and secure the openings with toothpicks.
5. Sprinkle the chops lightly with salt and pepper. Put the chops in a small baking pan and bake for 45 minutes. Turn the chops, increase the heat to 375 degrees, and bake for another 15 minutes, or until the chops are brown.

PORK CHOP AND EGGPLANT CASSEROLE

1 pork chop
   Salt and freshly ground black
   pepper
2 teaspoons flour
1 teaspoon dry mustard

1 tablespoon chopped onion
½ cup milk
1 small eggplant, trimmed and
   washed

1. Heat the oven to 375 degrees.
2. Trim the chop of most of its fat and the bone, if desired.
3. Sprinkle the chop with salt and pepper to taste and put it in an ovenproof casserole with a cover. Rub the chop over the bottom of the casserole to slightly grease the surface.
4. Combine the flour, mustard, onion, and milk and mix well.
5. Slice the eggplant into ¼-inch slices. Put the slices on top of the chop. Lightly salt and pepper the eggplant.
6. Pour the flour/milk mixture over the eggplant and add the butter in small pieces. Cover and bake for 1 hour. Serve hot.

PORK CHOP AND BAKED BEAN CASSEROLE

½ cup navy beans, picked over
   and washed
   Salt to taste
   Crushed red pepper flakes to
   taste
1 medium-sized onion, peeled
   and sliced
¼ cup ketchup

½ teaspoon wine vinegar
½ teaspoon dry mustard
1 tablespoon sorghum
1 center-cut pork chop
1 tablespoon bacon drippings or
   2 slices bacon
3 cups water

1. Put all ingredients in a heavy pot with a cover. The pork chop should be on top.
2. Bring to a boil and skim off any foam rising to the top.
3. Cover the pot and reduce the heat. Simmer for 3 to 3½ hours, or until the beans are tender. (If you soak the beans overnight before cooking, the cooking time can be reduced to 1½ hours, or until the beans are tender.)

PORK CHOP WITH CABBAGE

1 large or 2 small pork chops, trimmed of most fat
1 apple, cored and sliced but not peeled
1 onion, peeled, sliced, and broken into rings

1 ½-inch thick slice cabbage
¼ cup tomato purée
¼ cup chicken broth
Salt and freshly ground black pepper

1. Use a small skillet to brown the pork chop on both sides. Set the browned chop aside.
2. Preheat the oven to 300 degrees.
3. In a casserole with a cover make layers of apple slices, onion rings, and cabbage. Sprinkle each layer with salt and pepper to taste. Top the layers with the browned chop.
4. Combine the tomato purée and chicken broth. Mix well and pour over the pork chop. Sprinkle again with salt and pepper.
5. Cover the casserole and bake for 2½ hours. Uncover and bake a good sauce. Serve hot.
   for another 10 minutes, or until the liquid has reduced to make

BRAISED PORK AND TURNIP

2 pork chops, trimmed of fat and bone, or ¼ pound pork tenderloin
2 medium-sized turnips, peeled, washed, and sliced

¼ teaspoon dried thyme
Salt and freshly ground black pepper
2 tablespoons water

1. Brown the chops on both sides in a skillet over medium heat. Move the chops around to prevent sticking. Set aside.

2. Line the bottom of a small heavy pot with a cover with half the turnip slices. Put the browned chops on top of the turnips and cover with the remaining turnip slices. Add the thyme and salt and pepper to taste.
3. Pour the water into the skillet and stir to dissolve any browned juices clinging to the skillet. Add this liquid to the pork.
4. Cover the pot and put it over a Flame-Tamer over very low heat. Simmer for 1 hour. Serve hot.

PORK CHOP, SAUERKRAUT, AND APPLE CASSEROLE

1 pork chop	1 onion, peeled and finely
1 clove garlic, peeled and minced	chopped
Salt and freshly ground black	1 8-ounce can sauerkraut, drained
pepper	¼ cup sherry
½ red apple, cored and peeled	

1. Trim the chop of most of its fat. Put the trimmings in a small heavy pot with a cover. Render the fat and discard the solids.
2. Add the garlic to the pot and cook for 1 minute.
3. Sprinkle the trimmed chop with salt and pepper to taste and brown it on both sides in the grease in the pot. Remove the chop and set aside.
4. Line the pot with apple slices. Sprinkle the onion over the apple slices, and top with the drained sauerkraut. Put the chop on top of the sauerkraut and sprinkle it with more salt and pepper. Pour the sherry over all.
5. Cover the pot and put it over a Flame-Tamer over very low heat. Cook for 2 hours. This can also be baked at 350 degrees for 2 hours.

MILK-POACHED PORK CHOP

1 pork chop
Salt and freshly ground black
pepper to taste

Milk to cover

1. Salt a small skillet with a cover and brown the chop on both sides over medium-high heat.
2. Add pepper and cover the chop with milk.
3. Cover the skillet and put it on a Flame-Tamer over low heat. Simmer for 1 hour and serve hot.

PORK POT PIE

1 teaspoon vegetable oil
5 ounces boneless pork, cut into cubes
Pinch of dried thyme
Salt and freshly ground black pepper
1 carrot, trimmed, scraped, washed, and cut into small cubes
1 onion, peeled and cut into small cubes

1 small potato, peeled, washed, and cut into cubes
1 small inner stalk celery, trimmed, washed, and cut into small cubes
1 tablespoon water
2 teaspoons plus ¼ cup flour
½ teaspoon olive oil
½ teaspoon dry yeast
1 tablespoon lukewarm water

1. Heat the oil in a small saucepan. Add the pork and brown well. Sprinkle the pork with thyme and salt and pepper to taste and mix well.
2. Add the carrot, onion, potato, and celery. Sprinkle again with salt and pepper. Simmer for 15 minutes, or until the vegetables are almost tender.
3. Combine the water and 2 teaspoons of flour in a small cup and add it to the meat and vegetables. Stir well, remove from the heat, and set aside.

4. Prepare the crust: Put ¼ cup flour in a small bowl and add the olive oil. Use a small spatula or knife to work the oil into the flour. Mix well and eliminate any lumps.
5. Dissolve the yeast in the lukewarm water and stir the mixture into the dough. Work together until the dough pulls away from the sides of the bowl.
6. Cover the bowl and set it in a warm place, such as over a pilot light, for 15 minutes, or until the dough rises.
7. Knead the dough on a sheet of floured wax paper. Then flatten the dough out to form a cover for the pie.
8. Preheat the oven to 350 degrees.
9. Transfer the pork and vegetable mixture to a small ovenproof casserole. Top with the prepared crust. Press the crust against the sides of the casserole and make a steam slit in the center of the pastry.
10. Bake for 15 minutes. Then put the pie under the broiler for 5 minutes, or until the crust is browned.

DEVILED BACON

1 egg lightly beaten	2 teaspoons red wine vinegar
1 teaspoon dry mustard	4 slices bacon
½ teaspoon sugar	4 soda crackers, crumbled
Dash of Tabasco	

1. Preheat the oven to 475 degrees.
2. Blend the beaten egg, mustard, sugar, Tabasco, and vinegar in a shallow dish. Marinate the bacon slices in the mixture for 15 minutes, turning at least once.
3. Spread the cracker crumbs on a sheet of wax paper and coat both sides of the bacon strips with the crumbs.
4. Put the bacon on the rack in a roasting pan and bake until the bacon is crisp, about 10 minutes. Serve hot or cold.

CHINESE-STYLE MARINATED PORK

1 pork chop
2 teaspoons light soy sauce
½ teaspoon sugar
¼ teaspoon freshly ground black pepper

Salt to taste
1 teaspoon cornstarch
Vegetable oil for frying

1. Trim and discard the bone from the chop and remove any excess fat.
2. Pound the trimmed chop lightly on both sides.
3. Score the chop on both sides with a sharp knife.
4. In a shallow dish, combine the soy sauce, sugar, pepper, and salt.
5. Add the pork to the dish and marinate for at least 30 minutes, turning occasionally.
6. Drain the pork and sprinkle each side with half the cornstarch. Press the cornstarch into the meat.
7. Heat the oil in a skillet and, when it is quite hot, add the pork. Cover with a loose sheet of aluminum foil to curb the splashing oil, and cook over fairly high heat for 5 minutes on each side. Serve hot.

PORK CHOP AND APPLE CASSEROLE

1 pork chop, trimmed of most of its fat
1 apple, cored and sliced

Salt and freshly ground black pepper

1. Preheat the oven to 350 degrees.
2. Salt the bottom of a small casserole with a cover.
3. Sprinkle the chop on both sides with salt and pepper to taste and put it in the casserole. Arrange the apple slices on top of the chop.
4. Cover the casserole and bake for 1 hour. Serve the chop crowned with the cooked apple slices.

COUNTRY HAM STEAK WITH APPLE

1 country-cured ham steak   1 apple, cored and sliced

1. Score the edges of the ham steak to prevent curling and trim a bit of the bordering fat.
2. Over low heat fry the ham steak gently on one side for about 3 minutes.
3. Turn the ham and arrange the slices of apple on top of the ham slice. Continue cooking, covered with a sheet of aluminum foil. Cook for another 3 minutes or so, depending on the thickness of the ham. (This timing is for a thin, ¼-inch slice.)
4. Serve the ham very hot with the apple on top and with grits.

HAM AND BROCCOLI

2 cups broccoli flowerettes   3 or 4 ounces country ham, diced
   Salt   Lemon juice (optional)

1. Wash the broccoli flowerettes well and put them in a saucepan with water to cover. Add salt to taste. Bring to a boil and let them simmer for 4 minutes. Drain and set aside.
2. Put the diced ham over low heat in a skillet with a cover. Stir and turn for 4 minutes to cook the ham on all sides.
3. Add the drained broccoli flowerettes to the skillet and mix well. Cover and cook for 4 or 5 minutes, stirring occasionally. Serve hot with a dash of lemon juice, if desired.

BARBECUED PORK RIB ENDS

¾ pound pork rib ends with bones
Salt and freshly ground black
pepper
3 tablespoons ketchup
1 teaspoon lemon juice

¼ teaspoon Worcestershire sauce
¼ teaspoon Tabasco
1 tablespoon honey
1 tablespoon soy sauce

1. Preheat the oven to 350 degrees.
2. Sprinkle the rib ends with salt and pepper to taste. Put them on a rack in a baking pan.
3. Bake the rib ends for 30 minutes.
4. Mix the other ingredients together and coat the rib ends on one side. Return to the oven for another 30 minutes.
5. Turn the rib ends and coat the other side with the remaining sauce. Return to the oven and cook another 30 minutes.

HAM AND ASPARAGUS IN CHEESE SAUCE

5 spears fresh asparagus
2 teaspoons butter, plus butter
for the baking dish
¼ pound boneless cooked ham
2 teaspoons flour
½ cup milk

2 tablespoons grated Gruyere cheese
Salt and freshly ground black pepper
1 tablespoon grated Parmesan cheese

1. Preheat the oven to 400 degrees.
2. Peel the asparagus, using a potato peeler. Trim and discard the tough ends. Simmer the asparagus covered with salted water until just tender.
3. Grease a suitable small ovenproof dish and put the ham in the bottom. When the asparagus is barely tender, put it on top of the ham.

4. Make a roux by melting the 2 teaspoons of butter and stirring in the 2 teaspoons flour and, finally, the ½ cup milk. Stir continually until the sauce begins to thicken. Then stir in the Gruyere cheese and mix well. Taste for seasoning and add salt and pepper to your own taste.
5. Pour the cheese sauce over the ham and asparagus and top with the Parmesan cheese. Bake for 20 minutes. Put under the broiler for a minute or so if you want the top browned.

VEGETABLE CASSEROLE WITH HAM

1   teaspoon vegetable oil
1   carrot, trimmed, scraped, washed, and sliced
2   stalks celery, trimmed, washed, and sliced
1   small zucchini, trimmed, washed, and sliced
1   small onion, peeled and sliced
1   tablespoon minced parsley

1   small potato, peeled and sliced
½   cup diced cabbage
1   slice cooked ham or luncheon meat, cut into small cubes
1   small tomato, cored, washed, and sliced
    Salt and freshly ground black pepper

1. Heat the oil in a small heavy pot with a cover. Then remove the pot from the heat and tilt the pot to grease the bottom.
2. Make separate layers of the carrot, celery, zucchini, onion, parsley, potato, cabbage, and ham. Top with the tomato slices and sprinkle generously with salt and pepper.
3. Cover the pot and put it over very low heat. Cook until the vegetables are fork-tender. Serve hot.

HAM AND SQUASH CASSEROLE

1 small yellow squash, trimmed, washed, and sliced into ¼-inch slices
1 small onion, peeled and sliced

Salt and freshly ground black pepper
¼ pound country ham, sliced thin

1. Layer the squash slices in the bottom of a small heavy pot with a cover. Add the onion slices and salt and pepper to taste. Cover the onion slices with the sliced ham.
2. Cover the pot and simmer over very low heat for about 20 minutes, or until the vegetables are tender but not mushy. Serve the vegetables topped with the ham slices.

HAM LOAF

4 to 6 ounces country or other ham
1 stalk celery, trimmed and washed
1 small green pepper, cored, seeded, and washed

Freshly ground black pepper or crushed red pepper flakes to taste
1 egg
2 slices white bread, trimmed and cubed

1. Preheat the oven to 350 degrees.
2. Put all the ingredients into the container of a food processor or blender. Blend to a rather fine texture. If there is no food processor available, grind or chop all ingredients very small.
3. Line a baking pan with aluminum foil. Put the meat mixture into the pan and mold it into a loaf shape with a spatula. Cover the pan with aluminum foil.
4. Bake for 1 hour. Remove the foil for the last 15 minutes to allow a crust to form. Serve hot or cold, with or without sauce or relish.

Poultry

There is no better bargain in local markets today than chicken, and I enjoy it in many varied forms. Whether served in a cream sauce such as Brandied Chicken with Vegetables and Cream or Chicken Breast with Leeks in Cream Sauce; prepared with Red Wine Sauce or with Mushrooms and Pearl Onions in White Wine; or served in a London-style Chicken and Ham Pie, this versatile meat is sure to please.

I like turkey, too, and have included some of my favorite recipes in this chapter.

CHICKEN WITH POTATOES AND ROSEMARY

1 tablespoon olive oil
6 to 7 ounces raw chicken with bones
½ clove garlic, peeled and finely chopped
¼ cup dry white wine

1 teaspoon finely ground rosemary
½ bay leaf
1 cup potatoes, peeled, washed, and cut into ¼-inch slices
Salt and freshly ground black pepper

1. Preheat the oven to 400 degrees.
2. In a skillet with a cover, heat the oil to hot and sauté the chicken and garlic until the chicken is brown on both sides.
3. Pour off all but 1 tablespoon of oil and add the wine, rosemary, and bay leaf. Cover and cook for 5 minutes.
4. Add the potatoes and salt and pepper to taste. Cover again and bake for 25 minutes. Serve hot.

BAKED LEMON CHICKEN

1 tablespoon flour	2 teaspoons butter, melted
¼ teaspoon paprika	2 teaspoons lemon juice
Salt and freshly ground black pepper to taste (about ¼ teaspoon salt)	1 teaspoon olive oil
	1 teaspoon chopped shallots
	¼ clove garlic, peeled and minced
½ chicken breast	Pinch of dried thyme

1. Preheat oven to 375 degrees.
2. On a sheet of wax paper, combine the flour and paprika with salt and pepper to taste. Mix well and coat the chicken well.
3. Pour the melted butter into a small baking dish and turn the chicken in the melted butter to coat both sides.
4. Put the coated chicken skin side down in the baking dish, and bake for 20 minutes.
5. Mix together the lemon juice, olive oil, chopped shallots, garlic, and thyme.
6. Turn the chicken in the baking dish and pour the lemon juice mixture over it. Bake for another 20 minutes or until well browned. Serve hot.

COQ AU VIN

½ chicken breast	½ clove garlic, peeled and crushed
Flour for dredging	1 pinch dried thyme
Salt and freshly ground black pepper	1 sprig parsley
	½ bay leaf
1 tablespoon butter	6 whole small mushrooms
1 slice bacon, diced	1 ounce warm Cognac
6 small pearl onions, peeled and left whole	½ cup dry red wine

1. Preheat the oven to 300 degrees.
2. Mix the flour for dredging with salt and pepper to taste and coat the chicken on all sides.

3. Heat the butter in a skillet and brown the chicken on all sides. Transfer the chicken to a casserole with a cover, and add the diced bacon, onions, garlic, thyme, parsley, bay leaf, mushrooms, and a shake or so of additional salt and pepper. Pour the warm Cognac over all and ignite the liquor.
4. When the flame dies down, add the wine and cover the casserole. Bake for 2 hours, or until the chicken is quite tender.

CHICKEN WITH MUSHROOMS AND PEARL ONIONS IN WHITE WINE

	Salt and freshly ground black pepper	4	to 6 small mushrooms, stems removed
1	tablespoon flour or enough to dredge the chicken	6	small white pearl onions, peeled and left whole
½	chicken breast	¼	teaspoon dried thyme
1	tablespoon olive oil	½	bay leaf
		½	cup dry white wine

1. Preheat the oven to 350 degrees.
2. Mix the salt and pepper to taste with the flour on a sheet of wax paper and dredge the chicken breast on all sides.
3. Heat the oil in a skillet and brown the chicken on both sides. Remove it to a small casserole with a cover.
4. Add the mushrooms, onions, thyme, bay leaf, and white wine to the casserole. Sprinkle with more salt and pepper.
5. Cover the casserole and bake for 1 hour. Taste for doneness and seasoning, adding more salt and pepper, if necessary. Serve with rice or noodles.

CHICKEN BREAST VERONIQUE

½ chicken breast
2 tablespoons cracker crumbs
   Salt and freshly ground black
   pepper to taste
   Pinch dried tarragon

1 tablespoon butter
1 tablespoon chopped onion
2 tablespoons dry white wine
2 tablespoons chicken broth
⅓ cup seeded or seedless green
   grapes

1. Preheat the oven to 375 degrees.
2. Skin the chicken breast and coat both sides with cracker crumbs mixed with salt and pepper and tarragon.
3. Melt the butter in a skillet and brown the chicken on both sides. Transfer the chicken to a shallow baking dish.
4. Add the onion to the butter remaining in the skillet. Cook, stirring, until tender. Pour in the wine and broth and stir to dissolve any browned juices.
5. Pour the sauce over the chicken and bake, covered, for ½ hour. Add the grapes during the last 5 minutes. Serve hot.

CHICKEN BREAST BAKED ON POTATO-CARROT STUFFING

1 medium-sized carrot, trimmed,
   scraped, washed, and thinly
   sliced
1 medium-sized potato, peeled,
   washed, and cut into small
   pieces
   Salt and freshly ground pepper
4 teaspoons butter

1 small onion, peeled and
   chopped
1 stalk celery, trimmed, washed,
   and chopped
1 slice trimmed white bread,
   crumbled
1 egg
½ chicken breast

1. Put the carrot and potato in a saucepan and cover with salted water. Cook until tender. Drain and purée. Add 1 teaspoon butter and salt and pepper to taste.

2. Melt 1 teaspoon butter in a small skillet and add the onion and celery. Sauté for a few minutes.
3. Put the crumbled bread into a small bowl and add the sautéed onion and celery and the puréed potatoes and carrots and the egg. Mix well and season to taste with salt and pepper.
4. Preheat the oven to 375 degrees.
5. Put the vegetable-bread mixture into a small buttered casserole. Lay the chicken breast on top. Sprinkle the chicken breast lightly with salt and pepper. Dot with the remaining 2 teaspoons of butter. Bake, uncovered, for 40 minutes.

OVEN-BARBECUED CHICKEN

½ chicken breast
Salt and freshly ground black pepper
1 tablespoon tarragon vinegar
1 teaspoon Worcestershire sauce
1 teaspoon soy sauce
2 tablespoons ketchup or chili sauce
¼ cup chicken broth
Dash of Tabasco

1. Preheat the oven to 375 degrees.
2. Wipe the chicken off with a paper towel. Sprinkle lightly with salt and pepper.
3. Put the chicken skin side down in a casserole with a cover.
4. Mix the vinegar, Worcestershire sauce, soy sauce, ketchup, chicken broth, and Tabasco together in a bowl. Pour one half of the sauce over the chicken. Cover the casserole and bake for 15 minutes.
5. Turn the chicken over and moisten the exposed side with a little reserved sauce. Return the casserole, uncovered, to the oven and bake for another 40 minutes. Check occasionally and add more sauce to keep the chicken moist. Serve with rice, potatoes, noodles, or Yorkshire Pudding.

CHICKEN CACCIATORE—1

1 tablespoon olive oil
½ chicken breast
Salt
Paprika
1 small onion, peeled and chopped
1 clove garlic, peeled and crushed
1 stalk celery, trimmed, washed, and cut into ½-inch pieces

1 small Italian green pepper, cored, washed, seeded, and cut into 2-inch strips
1 medium-sized tomato, cored, peeled, and chopped
Pinch of dried thyme
Pinch of dried oregano
Pinch of dried basil

1. Heat the oil in a small skillet. Add the chicken and brown on all sides. Transfer the chicken to a small heavy pot with a cover. Sprinkle the chicken with salt and paprika.
2. In the oil remaining in the skillet, sauté the onion and garlic until wilted. Add the celery, green pepper, and tomato. Mix well. Season with thyme, oregano, and basil. Bring to a boil and pour over the chicken.
3. Simmer over very low heat for about 1 hour, or until the chicken and vegetables are tender. You may want to use a Flame-Tamer. You may prefer to bake the chicken at 350 degrees until it is tender. Serve with rice.

CHICKEN CACCIATORE—2

1 tablespoon olive oil
½ chicken breast
1 clove garlic, peeled and sliced
6 mushrooms, washed and sliced
¼ cup dry white wine
½ teaspoon dried rosemary

½ teaspoon dried basil
Salt and crushed red pepper flakes
⅓ cup peeled, seeded, and diced tomatoes

1. Heat the oil in a small heavy pot. Add the chicken and cook over very low heat, moving the chicken to coat it well with oil and to prevent it burning.
2. Add the garlic and cook over medium heat for 1 minute. Stir in the mushrooms.
3. Add the wine, rosemary, basil, and salt and crushed red pepper flakes to taste. Cover and simmer for 4 minutes.
4. Add the diced tomatoes. Cover and cook over low heat for another 30 minutes, or until the chicken is tender.

CHICKEN BREAST WITH MUSTARD SAUCE

½ chicken breast	2 teaspoons finely chopped shallots
Salt and freshly ground black pepper	2 teaspoons flour
2 teaspoons butter	¼ cup dry white wine
4 tiny carrots, trimmed, scraped, and washed	¼ cup chicken broth
6 small mushrooms, stems removed, washed and dried	½ bay leaf
	¼ teaspoon dried thyme
	2 teaspoons Dijon mustard

1. Sprinkle the chicken on both sides with salt and pepper to taste.
2. Melt the butter in a heavy skillet and sauté the chicken, skin side down, over medium-high heat, for 5 minutes, or until browned. Turn the chicken and brown on the other side.
3. Pour off the excess fat from the skillet and add the carrots, mushrooms, and shallots. Stir and cook for 4 or 5 minutes.
4. Sprinkle the flour over the chicken and vegetables, and stir to distribute it evenly. Add the wine, chicken broth, bay leaf, and thyme. Stir again. Cook, covered with aluminum foil, for 20 minutes. Baste and stir at least once at the beginning.
5. Remove the chicken from the heat and stir in the mustard. Serve immediately with rice.

CHICKEN WITH OLIVES

½ chicken breast
Salt and freshly ground black
pepper
2 teaspoons butter
4 or 5 medium-sized fresh
mushrooms with stems removed
1 tablespoon finely chopped
shallots

1 small clove garlic, peeled and
crushed
¼ cup dry white wine
½ cup canned Italian plum
tomatoes
¼ cup chicken broth
6 small pitted green olives or
small imported black olives

1. Sprinkle the chicken on all sides with salt and pepper to taste.
2. Melt the butter in a heavy skillet with a cover and sauté the chicken over medium heat for about 10 minutes, or until it is golden brown on all sides.
3. Rinse and quarter the mushrooms.
4. Remove the chicken from the skillet and add the mushrooms, shallots, and garlic. Stir and cook for 1 minute.
5. Add the wine, tomatoes, and broth. Cook and stir to dissolve any browned juices in the skillet. Cover and cook for 15 minutes over low heat.
6. Uncover and return the chicken to the sauce. Add the olives and cook, uncovered, for another 15 minutes. Serve hot with rice.

SKILLET CHICKEN

2 teaspoons butter
1 small onion, peeled and thinly
sliced
1 small green pepper, cored,
seeded, washed, and cut into
strips
Salt and freshly ground black
pepper

½ cup sliced mushrooms
1 teaspoon minced garlic
½ cup canned or fresh tomatoes
½ chicken breast, skinned
1 shallot, peeled and chopped
1 tablespoon dry white wine
1 tablespoon chicken broth
Parsley

1. Melt 1 teaspoon of butter in a small heavy pot. Add the onion and green pepper and sauté for 2 minutes. Season with salt and pepper to taste.
2. Add the mushrooms and cook another minute.
3. Add the garlic and tomatoes, and cook, over very low heat for 20 minutes, covered, or until the vegetables are tender. Uncover and continue cooking if there is too much liquid.
4. Melt the remaining teaspoon of butter in a skillet and sauté the chicken skin side down for 4 or 5 minutes, or until it is brown. Turn the chicken and brown the other side. Do not overcook.
5. Remove the chicken from the skillet and keep it warm. Add the chopped shallot to the skillet and cook, stirring, for 1 minute. Pour in the wine and cook until it is almost evaporated. Add the broth and stir to dissolve all browned juices in the pan.
6. Return the chicken to the skillet with the sauce and heat it through. Serve hot with rice.

CHICKEN BREAST WITH LEEKS IN CREAM SAUCE

½ chicken breast
1 cup trimmed, washed, and chopped leeks
1 stalk celery, trimmed, washed, and diced

½ teaspoon dried thyme
Water
Salt and freshly ground black pepper
1 tablespoon cream

1. Put the chicken, leeks, celery, and thyme in a saucepan with a cover. Add water to cover and season with salt and pepper to taste. Bring to a boil, cover, and simmer for 30 minutes.
2. Remove the chicken and keep it warm. Strain the liquid and boil it down to about ¼ cup. Add a bit of the strained vegetables for garnish.
3. Stir in the cream and return the chicken to the saucepan and heat through. Serve with rice.

CHICKEN IN RED WINE SAUCE

½ chicken breast
Salt and freshly ground black pepper
2 teaspoons butter
½ cup chopped mushrooms
2 tablespoons chopped shallots
1 clove garlic, peeled and finely minced

2 teaspoons flour
¼ cup dry red wine
2 tablespoons water or chicken broth
½ bay leaf
1 teaspoon chopped parsley
½ teaspoon dried thyme

1. Sprinkle the chicken on all sides with salt and pepper.
2. Melt the butter in a small heavy pot with a cover. Add the chicken skin side down, and brown over medium heat for about 6 minutes. Turn the chicken and cook on the other side for about 5 minutes.
3. Add the mushrooms, shallots, and garlic and stir and cook for 1 minute.
4. Sprinkle the flour evenly over the chicken and vegetables. Stir again.
5. Pour in the wine and water and add the bay leaf, parsley, and thyme. Cover and cook over low heat for 20 minutes, or until the chicken is tender. Serve hot.

CHICKEN WITH TOMATO AND CREAM SAUCE

½ chicken breast
Salt and freshly ground black pepper
2 teaspoons butter
1 teaspoon olive oil
1 tablespoon chopped shallots

1 medium-sized tomato, cored, peeled, and diced
1 tablespoon dry vermouth
Pinch of dried tarragon
2 tablespoons cream

1. Wipe the chicken with a dry cloth and sprinkle it lightly with salt and pepper.

2. Put the butter and olive oil in a skillet. When hot, add the chicken skin side down and sauté over medium heat for 5 minutes, or until brown. Turn the chicken, cover loosely with aluminum foil, and cook for 25 minutes.
3. When the chicken is tender, remove it to a warm place, cover with aluminum foil, and keep it warm.
4. Add the shallots to the fat remaining in the skillet. Cook, stirring, for 1 minute. Add the tomato, vermouth, and tarragon. Cook, stirring, for about 5 minutes. Stir in the cream and taste for seasonings, adding salt and pepper, if necessary. Pour the warm sauce over the chicken and serve immediately.

MEXICAN CHICKEN

½ chicken breast
Salt and freshly ground black pepper
2 teaspoons olive oil
1 teaspoon chopped onion
1 clove garlic, peeled and crushed
2 tablespoons dry sherry

1 teaspoon chili powder
¼ teaspoon ground cumin
¼ teaspoon dried oregano, crushed
2 teaspoons flour
1 small tomato, peeled, cored, and chopped
5 pitted green olives

1. Sprinkle the chicken with salt and pepper. Heat the oil in a skillet and brown the chicken on both sides. Transfer the chicken to a small heavy pot with a cover.
2. Add the onion, garlic, and sherry to the fat in the skillet. Stir and cook down so very little liquid remains.
3. Sprinkle in the chili powder, cumin, oregano, and flour. Blend well and stir in the chopped tomato. Stir until thickened. If the tomato is not providing enough liquid to form a medium sauce, add more sherry and stir again.
4. Pour the sauce over the chicken, cover, and simmer for 30 minutes, or until the chicken is tender.
5. Add the olives and serve hot.

BRANDIED CHICKEN WITH VEGETABLES AND CREAM

½ chicken breast
Salt and freshly ground black pepper
2 tablespoons butter
2 tablespoons Cognac
1 small potato, peeled and diced
1 small turnip, peeled and diced

1 small carrot, trimmed, scraped, washed, and diced
1 small white onion, chopped
1 small zucchini, trimmed, washed, and diced
8 green beans, trimmed and cut into ½-inch lengths
3 tablespoons cream

1. Sprinkle the chicken with salt and pepper and sauté it in 1 tablespoon of the butter over low heat for 10 minutes on the skin side. Turn and sauté on the other side until brown.
2. Add the Cognac to the chicken and cover and simmer for 10 minutes. Do not burn. Watch the heat and keep it low.
3. Put the vegetables in a saucepan and cover with water. Add salt and pepper and bring to a boil. Cook for 1 minute and drain in a sieve or colander.
4. Add the remaining butter to the saucepan in which the vegetables were cooked and return the drained vegetables to the saucepan. Stir, toss, and cook the vegetables, covered, for 5 minutes.
5. Add the vegetables to the chicken and pour in the cream. Bring to a boil and cook slowly over low heat for about 6 minutes.

ARROZ CON POLLO

½ chicken breast
2 teaspoons olive oil
½ clove garlic, peeled and minced
1 teaspoon chopped parsley
2 tablespoons raw rice

⅓ cup water
2 teaspoons drained capers
1 tablespoon sliced, stuffed olives
Crushed red pepper flakes
Salt

1. Wipe the chicken with a paper towel and set aside.
2. Heat the oil in a small heavy pot with a cover. Add the chicken and brown it on both sides.
3. Add the garlic and parsley and stir in. Add the rice and stir and cook until it is golden. Pour in the water. Reduce the heat, cover, and simmer until the rice is cooked.
4. Add the capers and olives and season the dish with crushed red pepper flakes and salt, if necessary. Serve hot.

CHICKEN IN TARRAGON-CREAM SAUCE

½ chicken breast
1 tablespoon lemon juice
1 carrot, trimmed, scraped, washed, and sliced
1 stalk celery, trimmed, washed, and sliced
1 leek, trimmed, washed well, and sliced
1 small onion, peeled and sliced
¼ teaspoon dried tarragon
½ bay leaf
3 whole peppercorns
  Salt
  Water
2 teaspoons butter
2 teaspoons flour
1 tablespoon light cream

1. Marinate the chicken in the lemon juice for at least 20 minutes.
2. Put the chicken in a covered saucepan. Add the carrot, celery, leek, onion, tarragon, bay leaf, peppercorns, and salt to taste. Add water to cover the chicken.
3. Bring to a boil, cover, lower the heat, and simmer for 30 minutes, or until the chicken is tender.
4. Remove the chicken and keep it warm. Reserve a slice or two of carrot and onion for garnish.
5. Pass the liquid and the remaining vegetables through a sieve pressing as much of the vegetables through as you can. Discard the remaining vegetables.
6. Boil the strained liquid down to about ½ cup over high heat. In a small saucepan, melt the butter and add the flour. Stir well and add the reduced stock. Stir until thickened.
7. Add the cream and mix well. Serve over the chicken and garnish with the reserved carrot and onion. Serve with rice.

BRAISED CHICKEN WITH TRUFFLES

½ breast of chicken
Salt and freshly ground
black pepper to taste

1 tablespoon butter
¼ cup chicken broth
½ teaspoon finely chopped truffles

1. Sprinkle the chicken with salt and pepper.
2. Melt the butter in a small skillet and brown the chicken on the skin side for about 4 minutes and on the other side for 2 or 3 minutes.
3. Transfer the browned chicken breast to a small heavy pot with a cover.
4. Pour the chicken broth over the chicken and scatter the chopped truffles over the chicken.
5. Cover the pot and simmer over low heat for about 20 minutes, or until the chicken is fork-tender.
6. Put the chicken on a hot plate and keep it warm. Turn up the flame under the pot and reduce the liquid to about 1 tablespoon. Pour the reduced broth over the chicken and serve.

Note: Unused truffles can be kept covered by oil in a closed jar in the refrigerator. They will keep some time, at least a few months, and can be used in fillet with truffles, scrambled eggs, Sauce Perigordine, etc.

BREADED CHICKEN BREAST—1

½ chicken breast, skinned and
boned
1 tablespoon flour
Salt and freshly ground black
pepper

1 egg yolk
1 teaspoon water
¼ cup bread crumbs
1 tablespoon vegetable oil
1 slice lemon

1. Put the chicken cutlet between two sheets of wax paper and pound it lightly with a meat mallet.

2. Dredge both sides of the chicken in flour, mixed with salt and pepper to taste.
3. Beat the egg yolk and water in a saucer. Coat both sides of the chicken in the egg mixture and then in bread crumbs. Pat the chicken to make the bread crumbs stick.
4. Heat the oil in a skillet and add the chicken. Cook the chicken over medium heat for about 3 or 4 minutes on each side, or until the chicken is golden brown.
5. Serve hot with lemon slice on top. You may enjoy a wedge of lemon also.

BREADED CHICKEN BREAST—2

½ chicken breast, skinned and boned
Salt and freshly ground black pepper

2 slices trimmed white bread in crumbs
1 egg
1 tablespoon butter
1 tablespoon vegetable oil

1. Remove any skin and bone fragments from the chicken cutlet. Pound the cutlet lightly between sheets of wax paper, using a meat mallet. Sprinkle the chicken lightly with salt and pepper.
2. Put the bread crumbs in a flat plate. Beat the egg well in a second plate.
3. Dip the pounded chicken in the egg and then in the crumbs. Turn in both dishes and coat well with both ingredients. Repeat the process and incorporate most of the egg and crumbs.
4. Put the butter and oil in a skillet. When they are quite hot, add the chicken and reduce the heat to moderate to low. Cook the chicken for 2½ to 3 minutes on each side. Serve hot.

BREAST OF CHICKEN WITH
VEGETABLE JULIENNE

½ chicken breast, skinned and boned
Salt and freshly ground black pepper to taste
3 teaspoons butter
1 teaspoon flour
⅓ cup chicken broth

1 small carrot, trimmed, scraped, washed, and cut in very fine strips
1 rib celery, trimmed, washed, and cut into very fine strips
¼ cup finely shredded fresh mushrooms
2 tablespoons cream

1. Sprinkle the chicken with salt and pepper and set aside.
2. Melt 1 teaspoon butter in a saucepan and add the flour. Stir and mix well and add the chicken broth. Stir again and cook over low heat for 10 minutes. Set aside.
3. In another saucepan, with a cover, melt 1 teaspoon butter and add the carrot, celery, and mushrooms. Cover the pan and wilt the vegetables over low heat for about 6 to 7 minutes.
4. In a skillet with a cover, melt the remaining butter and brown the chicken on both sides.
5. Scatter the vegetables over the chicken and cover the skillet. Cook for 10 minutes over moderate heat. Remove the chicken and keep it warm.
6. Stir the cream into the skillet juices and return the chicken to the mixture. Add the reserved sauce and heat through. Serve with rice, noodles, or mashed potatoes.

CHICKEN BREAST FLORENTINE

½ of a 10-ounce package of fresh spinach
½ chicken breast, skinned and boned
Salt and freshly ground black pepper
2 teaspoons butter
1 tablespoon finely chopped shallots

¼ cup dry white wine
¼ cup chicken broth
1 tablespoon chopped parsley
2 teaspoons flour
¼ cup light cream
1 egg yolk
1 tablespoon grated Parmesan cheese

1. Wash the spinach well in cold water and put it in a saucepan with tight-fitting cover. Turn the pan and drain off the excess water which does not cling to the spinach. Cover tightly and place over the lowest heat. Let the spinach melt or wilt completely over very low heat. This may take 1 hour.
2. Put the chicken breast between sheets of wax paper and pound it with a meat mallet. Sprinkle it with salt and pepper.
3. Melt 1 teaspoon of butter and grease a skillet with a cover. Sprinkle the bottom of the skillet with the chopped shallots. Put the chicken on the shallots and pour in the wine and chicken broth. Add the parsley.
4. Melt the remaining teaspoon of butter and mix in the flour.
5. Bring the chicken and liquids and seasonings to a boil and simmer, covered, for 20 minutes. Remove the chicken and reserve the liquid.
6. Pour the reserved liquid into the flour and butter mixture over low heat and stir until it begins to thicken. Remove from the heat and quickly stir in the egg yolk. Cook for 1 or 2 minutes. Taste for seasonings and add salt, if necessary.
7. Preheat the broiler.
8. Put the spinach in a baking dish and lay the chicken on top of it. Pour the thickened sauce over all. Sprinkle the cheese on top. Put under the broiler until bubbling and lightly browned.

CHICKEN MOGUL

½ chicken breast
Salt and freshly ground black
  pepper to taste
½ cup chicken broth
1 small onion, peeled

1 small tomato, cored, peeled,
  and seeded
½ teaspoon curry powder
½ teaspoon turmeric
1 tablespoon plain yogurt

1. Sprinkle the chicken breast with salt and pepper. Put it in a saucepan with a cover. Add the chicken broth and the peeled onion. Bring to a boil, cover, and simmer for 30 minutes. Let the chicken cool. Then bone and skin it and cut it into bite-sized pieces. Discard the bones and skin.
2. Place the seeded and peeled tomato and ½ cup of the liquid in which the chicken was cooked in the container of a food processor or blender. Turn the processor on and off to prepare a thin, smooth sauce. The sauce will be smoother if you strain the liquid before adding it. If there is no food processor available, press the tomato and the liquid through a sieve.
3. Return the sauce to the saucepan. Season the sauce with curry powder and turmeric. Mix well and bring to a boil. Remove from the heat and stir in the yogurt until blended.
4. Taste for seasonings and add more of any of the seasonings desired.
5. Add the chicken to the sauce. Blend well and heat through. Serve with rice.

POACHED CHICKEN WITH CARROTS

6 to 8 ounces boned and skinned chicken
Salt and freshly ground black pepper
¾ cup jullienned carrots

¼ cup dry white wine
½ cup chicken broth
2 teaspoons flour
1 teaspoon butter

1. Sprinkle the chicken with salt and pepper. Put the chicken in a small heavy pot with a cover. Add the carrots and sprinkle them with salt and pepper. Pour in the wine and chicken broth.
2. Bring to a boil, cover, and simmer for about 20 minutes. Remove the chicken and carrots and keep warm.
3. Mix the flour and butter together into a paste.
4. Using high heat, reduce the liquid in which the chicken and carrots cooked to about ¼ cup. Add the flour and butter mixture a little at a time, until the sauce thickens.
5. Return the chicken and carrots to the sauce and heat through.

CHICKEN BREAST WITH BOURBON-CREAM SAUCE

Flour for dredging
Salt and freshly ground black pepper to taste
½ chicken breast, skinned and boned

1 tablespoon butter
1 tablespoon chopped shallots
1 tablespoon Bourbon whiskey
3 tablespoons cream
Dash of Tabasco

1. Mix the flour and salt and pepper on a sheet of wax paper and dredge the chicken on both sides.
2. Melt the butter in a skillet and, when hot, brown the chicken for about 4 or 5 minutes on each side.
3. Remove the chicken and add the shallots to the skillet. Cook for 1 minute and add the whiskey and then the cream. Boil for a minute and season with Tabasco and more salt, if necessary.

CHICKEN IN CHAMPAGNE SAUCE

½ chicken breast
1 small carrot, trimmed, scraped, washed, and sliced
2 inner stalks celery, trimmed, washed, and sliced
½ teaspoon dried thyme
Water or chicken broth

Salt and freshly ground black pepper
1 teaspoon butter
1 teaspoon flour
¼ cup champagne
¼ teaspoon sugar

1. Put the chicken in a saucepan with a cover. Add the carrot, celery, and dried thyme. Cover with water or broth and season with salt and pepper to taste. Bring to a boil, cover, reduce the heat, and simmer for 1 hour.
2. Remove the chicken, cut it into bite-sized pieces, and keep it warm. The cooking liquid and vegetables can be puréed and made into soup.
3. Prepare the champagne sauce: Melt the butter in a small saucepan. Stir in the flour and cook for 1 minute. Pour in the champagne slowly, stirring constantly. Season with sugar and add the reserved chicken and heat through.

CHINESE-STYLE POACHED CHICKEN BREAST

½ chicken breast at room temperature
Water
1 tablespoon vegetable oil
1 tablespoon finely shredded fresh ginger

5 small scallions, trimmed, washed, and cut into ¼-inch lengths
1 tablespoon light soy sauce
½ teaspoon sugar
Salt to taste
2 teaspoons dry sherry

1. Put the chicken in a saucepan and cover it with water. Bring the water to a boil, reduce the heat, and simmer for 25 minutes. Let the chicken cool in the liquid in which it was cooked.
2. When the chicken is cool enough to handle, skin and bone it, and cut it into bite-sized pieces.

3. Heat the oil in a wok or skillet and sauté the ginger and scallions for 1 minute, stirring constantly.
4. Add the soy sauce, sugar, salt, and sherry.
5. Bring the sauce to a boil, stirring, and add the chicken. Mix to coat the chicken well, and heat through. Serve with rice.

LONDON-STYLE CHICKEN AND HAM PIE

½   chicken breast
1   small onion, peeled and cut in half
1   small carrot, trimmed, scraped, washed, and sliced
½   teaspoon dried thyme
Salt and freshly ground black pepper

Water to cover the chicken
2   teaspoons flour
2   tablespoons water
1   thin slice ham, diced
Pastry crust (see recipe page 231)

1. Put the chicken breast in a saucepan with the onion, carrot, thyme, and salt and pepper to taste. Add water to almost cover. Bring to a boil and simmer for 1 hour. Let the chicken cool in the liquid in which it was cooked.
2. When the chicken is cool enough to handle, skin and bone it, and cut the meat into small chunks.
3. Remove the vegetables from the cooking liquid and set them aside.
4. Reduce the cooking liquid by about one half by boiling it over high heat.
5. Mix the flour and water together in a small cup and add the mixture to the reduced liquid. Stir over low heat, until the sauce thickens. Add the reserved chicken and vegetables and the diced ham to the sauce.
6. Preheat the oven to 400 degrees.
7. Put the chicken and ham mixture in a baking dish and cover the dish with the pastry crust. Bake for ½ hour. Brown the crust under the broiler, if necessary, and serve immediately.

DICED CHICKEN AND MUSHROOMS

½ chicken breast
Water
Salt
1 tablespoon chopped shallots
6 fresh mushrooms

1 tablespoon butter
½ clove garlic, peeled and minced
2 teaspoons flour
2 tablespoons chopped parsley

1. Put the chicken breast in a saucepan with water to cover, salt to taste, and a few of the chopped shallots. Bring to a boil, lower the heat, and simmer for 30 minutes. Let the chicken cool in the liquid in which it was cooked. Reserve the cooking liquid.
2. When cool enough to handle, skin, bone, and dice the chicken.
3. Remove the stems from the mushrooms and set them aside for another use. Peel and slice the mushroom caps in thick slices.
4. Melt the butter in a small skillet and add the remaining shallots and the garlic. Sauté for 1 minute. Sprinkle the flour over the vegetables and mix well. Pour in ¼ cup of the cooking liquid. Stir and mix until the sauce is thickened.
5. Add the diced chicken and the mushrooms. Heat through. Serve over toast or with rice, sprinkled with parsley.

CHICKEN IN PIMIENTO-CREAM SAUCE

½ chicken breast
Salt and freshly ground black pepper
¼ teaspoon dried thyme
½ bay leaf
1 tablespoon chopped onion

Water
1 teaspoon butter
1½ teaspoons flour
2 tablespoons cream
2 tablespoons chopped pimiento

1. Put the chicken, salt and pepper to taste, thyme, bay leaf, and onion in a small pot with a cover. Add water to cover. Bring to a boil, cover, and simmer for 25 minutes, or until the chicken is fork-tender. Let the chicken cool in the cooking liquid.

2. When the chicken is cool, remove it, bone and skin it, and cut it into bite-sized pieces.
3. Boil the chicken cooking liquid down over high heat until it is reduced to about ¼ cup.
4. In a small saucepan, melt the butter and stir in the flour. Cook for 1 minute, stirring, and add the ½ cup reduced liquid. Mix well and add the cream. Add the chicken to the sauce with the pimientos. Taste for seasonings and adjust, if necessary. Serve with rice or boiled potatoes.

CHICKEN AND MUSHROOMS
IN MUSTARD SAUCE

½ chicken breast, cooked
⅓ cup cooking liquid from chicken or chicken broth
1 teaspoon Dijon mustard
Salt and freshly ground black pepper

2 teaspoons flour
3 tablespoons chopped fresh tomato
6 medium-sized mushroom caps, washed and dried

1. Skin and bone the cooked chicken and cut it into bite-sized pieces.
2. Heat the cooking liquid and stir in the mustard and salt and pepper to taste.
3. Put the chicken on a sheet of wax paper and sprinkle it with flour. Coat well.
4. Add the coated chicken to the sauce and blend well. Then add the tomato and the mushrooms. Stir and heat through. Serve with rice or puréed potatoes.

CHICKEN AND ASPARAGUS—1

6 asparagus spears	Salt and freshly ground black
½ chicken breast	pepper
Water	2 teaspoons butter
½ teaspoon dried thyme	2 teaspoons flour
1 clove garlic, peeled and sliced	1 teaspoon curry powder
1 stalk celery, trimmed, washed,	(optional)
and sliced	Butter
½ bay leaf	2 saltine crackers, crumbled
1 slice lemon	

1. Peel and trim the asparagus, and cut them into ½-inch lengths. Cook in salted water to cover until just tender. Drain and set aside, but reserve the cooking liquid.
2. Put the chicken breast in a saucepan with water to cover. Add thyme, garlic, celery, bay leaf, lemon, and salt and pepper to taste. Bring to a boil, lower the heat, and cook until just tender. Let the chicken cool in the cooking liquid.
3. When cool enough to handle, skin and bone the chicken. Cut into bite-sized pieces and set aside.
4. Combine the cooking liquids from the asparagus and chicken. Reduce them to about ½ cup by boiling over high heat. Set aside.
5. In a small skillet, melt the butter and stir in the flour and curry powder, if desired. Add the ½ cup reserved liquid and stir until smooth and thick.
6. Preheat the oven to 350 degrees.
7. Butter the sides and bottom of a small baking dish. Put the reserved asparagus on the bottom. Top the asparagus with the reserved chicken pieces. Pour the sauce over the chicken and sprinkle the crumbled crackers over all.
8. Bake, uncovered, for 30 minutes. Serve hot.

CHICKEN AND ASPARAGUS—2

6 to 7 ounces boneless chicken, cut into bite-sized pieces
1 cup peeled and trimmed asparagus, cut into ½-inch lengths
1 small white onion, peeled and thinly sliced
¼ teaspoon dried thyme
1 cup chicken broth
Salt and freshly ground black pepper
1 teaspoon butter
2 teaspoons flour
1 tablespoon grated Parmesan cheese

1. Put the chicken, asparagus, onion, thyme, and broth into a saucepan. Season with salt and pepper to taste. Bring to a boil, lower the heat, and simmer for 20 minutes. Remove the chicken, asparagus, and onion and put them in a baking dish.
3. Boil down the cooking liquid until it is reduced to about ¼ cup.
4. Mix the butter and flour together and stir into the reduced liquid, bit by bit, to thicken it. Taste the sauce, and add more salt, if necessary.
5. Pour the sauce over the chicken and vegetables in the baking dish. Sprinkle with cheese and put the dish under the broiler for 2 or 3 minutes, or until the liquid is bubbling.

POACHED CHICKEN WINGS WITH LEEK

3 chicken wings
1 leek, cleaned and sliced
3 small carrots, trimmed, scraped, washed, and sliced
1 small white onion, peeled and halved
1 stalk celery, trimmed, washed, and sliced
½ teaspoon dried thyme
Salt and freshly ground black pepper
1½ cups chicken broth

1. Put the chicken wings, leek, carrots, onion, celery, thyme, and salt and pepper to taste in a medium-sized saucepan with a cover.
2. Add the chicken broth, which should just about cover the ingredients. Bring to a boil, cover the pan, lower the heat, and simmer for 1 hour.
3. Remove the chicken wings and keep them warm. Leave the vegetables in the pan and pour off all but ¾ cup of the cooking liquid. The extra liquid can be reserved for another use. Bring the ¾ cup cooking liquid to a boil, and boil until it is reduced by half.
4. Return the chicken wings to the pan and heat through. Serve hot.

POACHED CHICKEN WINGS WITH PRUNES AND APRICOTS

3 dried prunes
3 dried apricots
Water
1 tablespoon sugar
3 chicken wings or ½ chicken breast
1 tablespoon flour
½ teaspoon salt
1 tablespoon vegetable oil
¾ cup chicken broth
1 teaspoon brown sugar
1 tablespoon water

1. Put the dried fruit in a saucepan and cover with water. Add 1 tablespoon sugar and bring to a boil. Cook for 1 minute and turn off the heat. Let the fruit stand in the hot water until needed.

2. If you are using chicken wings, cut off and discard the small wing tip. Cut the wing in half at the joint.
3. Combine the flour and salt on a sheet of wax paper. Use this mixture to flour the chicken on all sides. Reserve any leftover flour mixture for later.
4. Heat the oil in a small skillet with a cover. Add the chicken pieces and brown on all sides.
5. Add the drained prunes and apricots, chicken broth, and brown sugar. Bring to a boil, cover, reduce the heat, and simmer for 45 minutes, or until the chicken is well cooked.
6. Mix together the reserved flour mixture from step 3 with 1 tablespoon of water. Add this to the casserole and mix well. Taste, and add salt, if necessary. Serve hot.

CHICKEN HASH

2 teaspoons butter	¼ cup diced green pepper
¼ pound raw chicken, cut into small cubes	2 tablespoons light cream
	1 egg yolk
1 small white onion, peeled and chopped	Salt and freshly ground black pepper
1 small tomato, cored, peeled, and chopped	4 stuffed olives, sliced
	1 hard-cooked egg, diced
1 small potato, peeled and diced	

1. Melt the butter in a small saucepan with a cover. Add the chicken cubes and the onion and stir and cook for 1 or 2 minutes.
2. Add the tomato, potato, and green pepper and mix well. Cover, reduce the heat, and simmer for 10 minutes.
3. Mix the cream and egg yolk and stir into the hash. Season with salt and pepper to taste.
4. Gently add the sliced olives and diced egg and heat through. Serve with rice, couscous, grits, or corn bread.

CHICKEN LOAF

⅔ cup cooked, skinned, and   Salt and freshly ground black
    boned chicken   pepper
2 tablespoons bread crumbs   ¼ teaspoon paprika
1 egg yolk   ¼ cup chicken broth
                                  Butter

1. Preheat the oven to 350 degrees.
2. Grind or finely chop the chicken.
3. Combine the chicken, bread crumbs, egg yolk, salt and pepper to taste, paprika, and chicken broth. Mix well.
4. Butter a small baking dish and put the chicken mixture into it. Bake for 40 minutes. Serve with Mushroom Sauce (see recipe page 211) or your favorite sauce.

HOLIDAY TURKEY BREAST

1½ pounds turkey breast at room   1 tablespoon butter
    temperature   ¼ cup brandy
    Salt and freshly ground black
    pepper

1. Wipe the turkey with a cloth and remove any pin feathers or extraneous matter. Sprinkle the breast on both sides with salt and pepper to taste. Rub the skin side with butter.
2. Preheat the oven to 300 degrees.
3. Line a small baking pan with aluminum foil. Put the seasoned breast skin side up in the center of the pan.
4. Bake for ½ hour. Pour the brandy over and cover the turkey with a sheet of aluminum foil. Bake for another ½ hour, basting frequently. Test to see that the meat is done; if it is not, cook it a little longer. Slice thinly and serve wih the pan gravy.

Note: This quantity of turkey should make two servings, with a little left over for cold sandwiches.

TURKEY WITH CREAMED CORN AND GREEN PEPPER

1 8½-ounce can cream-style corn
½ cup chopped green pepper

¼ pound cooked turkey breast, cut into bite-sized pieces
Salt and freshly ground black pepper to taste

1. Put all the ingredients into a small saucepan with a cover. Simmer, covered, over low heat for 1 hour.
2. Taste for seasonings, and add more salt and pepper, if necessary. Serve hot.

TURKEY HASH

2 teaspoons butter
1 small white onion, peeled and chopped
2 tablespoons chopped green pepper
2 tablespoons diced tomatoes

Salt and freshly ground black pepper
1 teaspoon flour
½ cup chicken broth
2½ to 3 ounces cooked turkey, cut into bite-sized pieces
2 large stuffed olives, sliced

1. Melt the butter in a small saucepan and sauté the onion over low heat for 1 minute, or until it is wilted.
2. Add the green pepper and diced tomato and stir well. Season with salt and pepper to taste.
3. Stir in the flour and mix well. Cook for 1 minute and add the chicken broth. Stir until the sauce begins to thicken.
4. Mix in the cooked turkey and heat. Add the sliced olives and serve hot with rice.

Fish and Shellfish

Although I never liked to eat fish when I was growing up, all I had to do was try fresh fish from the east coast once, and the appeal was there. In recent years, I have learned several enjoyable fish recipes for individual servings of flounder, salmon, tuna, sole, and cod, as well as shellfish like lobster, crabs, shrimp, and oysters. Some of my favorites from the recipes which follow include Flounder with Tomato and Green Pepper Sauce, Dilled Salmon Steak, Italian-style Tuna, and Shrimp with Capers and Dill.

SAUTEED FISH FILLET WITH CAPERS AND LEMON

¼ pound filleted sole or flounder
2 tablespoons milk
Salt and freshly ground pepper
½ small lemon
2 tablespoons flour

2 tablespoons vegetable oil
2 teaspoons butter
1 teaspoon drained capers
1 teaspoon finely chopped parsley

1. Soak the fish in the milk seasoned with salt and pepper to taste. Coat well on both sides and let stand.
2. Peel and trim the lemon to remove all white pulp and yellow skin. Slice the lemon thinly and remove any seeds. Cut the slices into small cubes and set aside.
3. Put the flour on a sheet of wax paper and season it with salt.
4. Heat the oil and 1 teaspoon of the butter in a skillet large enough to hold the fish in one flat position.

5. Remove the fish from the milk and coat both sides lightly with flour. Shake off any excess flour.
6. When the oil is hot, but not smoking, add the fish and cook to a golden brown on one side and turn and do the other side. Remove the fish to a warm platter.
7. In the remaining 1 teaspoon of butter, cook and stir the lemon and capers for a minute or so and pour over the fish. Sprinkle with chopped parsley and serve immediately.

COD FILLET WITH POTATOES, ONION, AND BREAD CRUMBS

2 small potatoes, peeled, washed, and thinly sliced

1 small onion, peeled, thinly sliced, and separated into rings

3 teaspoons butter

1 fillet (about ⅓ pound) cod

Salt and freshly ground black pepper

1 tablespoon chopped parsley

½ clove garlic, peeled and minced

3 tablespoons bread crumbs

2 tablespoons dry white wine

1. Preheat the oven to 425 degrees.
2. Cover the potatoes with cold water and set aside.
3. Melt 1 teaspoon of the butter and butter the bottom of a small baking dish.
4. Add the cod and sprinkle it with salt and pepper to taste.
5. Drain the sliced potatoes and put them in a mixing bowl with the onion rings, garlic, and salt and pepper to taste. Sprinkle with parsley and blend well.
6. Arrange the vegetables around the fillet in the baking dish. Dot them with the remaining butter. Sprinkle the cod fillet with the bread crumbs and moisten it with the wine.
7. Bake for 30 minutes and serve immediately.

FILLET OF FLOUNDER WITH TOMATO AND GREEN PEPPER

3 teaspoons olive oil
½ cup chopped green pepper
2 tablespoons chopped onion
1 medium-sized ripe tomato, cored, peeled, and chopped or ⅔ cup canned tomatoes, chopped

1 tablespoon chopped parsley
1 teaspoon dried basil
Salt and freshly ground black pepper
1 flounder fillet

1. Preheat the broiler.
2. Heat 2 teaspoons olive oil in a saucepan and sauté the pepper and onion until the onion is translucent. Add the tomato, parsley, basil, and salt and pepper to taste. Mix well and simmer until the pepper is tender. Transfer the sauce to a baking dish large enough to accommodate the fish.
3. Oil the flounder on both sides with the remaining oil and arrange it on the sauce in the baking dish.
4. Broil under medium-high heat for 7 minutes. Turn up the heat to high and continue to broil for 3 minutes, or until the flounder begins to brown on top. Serve hot.

BAKED FLOUNDER WITH FRESH ASPARAGUS AND POTATOES

2 small potatoes, peeled
1 tablespoon olive oil
1 flounder fillet
1 clove garlic, peeled and minced

1 teaspoon chopped mint
Salt and freshly ground black pepper
½ pound fresh asparagus
1 teaspoon dried basil
Juice of ½ lemon

1. Peel the potatoes and boil in salted water until almost cooked, about 15 minutes. Drain and set aside.

2. Preheat the oven to 450 degrees.
3. Pour the olive oil into an ovenproof vessel and add the flounder fillet. Turn the fish several times to coat with oil.
4. Sprinkle the fish with minced garlic, mint, and salt and pepper to taste.
5. Put the peeled and trimmed asparagus in the baking dish alongside the fish. Sprinkle with dried basil and lemon juice.
6. Slice the partially cooked potatoes and arrange them around the fish and asparagus in the baking dish.
7. Bake for 20 minutes, or until the asparagus and potatoes are fork-tender. Serve hot.

BAKED FISH FILLET AND BROCCOLI

1 cup washed and trimmed broccoli flowerettes	2 tablespoons dry white wine
1 tablespoon butter	2 tablespoons heavy or light cream
1 tablespoon chopped shallots	Salt and freshly ground black pepper to taste
6 ounces or so of skinless, boneless fillet of flounder or other white fish	

1. Preheat the oven to 475 degrees.
2. Place the broccoli in a saucepan with water to cover and salt to taste. Bring to a boil and simmer for 4 minutes. Drain and set aside.
3. Melt the butter in a flameproof casserole that will accommodate the fillet. First sauté the chopped shallots for 1 minute, stirring constantly. Then place the fillet of fish on the sautéed shallots. Heat on top of the stove until the butter begins to boil. Pour the wine and the cream over the fish. Immediately arrange the broccoli flowerettes around and on the fillet. Cover with aluminum foil and bake for 15 minutes. Serve hot.

BAKED LEMON SOLE

1 teaspoon olive oil	3 tablespoons dry white wine
3 teaspoons butter	1 tablespoon lemon juice
2 large mushrooms, chopped	Salt
1 tablespoon chopped shallots	Lemon wedges
¼ to ½ pound filleted lemon sole	

1. Preheat the oven to 350 degrees.
2. Put the oil and 1 teaspoon of the butter in an ovenproof baking dish. Melt these and coat the bottom of the dish.
3. Sprinkle the bottom of the dish with one half the mushrooms and one half the chopped shallots. Cover this base with the sole. Top the fish with the remaining mushrooms and shallots. Dot the top with the remaining butter.
4. Mix the wine and lemon juice and pour the liquid over all. Salt the dish to taste and bake for 20 minutes, or until the fish flakes easily. Serve hot.

FILLET OF SOLE WITH TOMATOES

1 fillet (6 to 7 ounces) of sole or flounder	2 tablespoons drained and chopped canned tomatoes
2 teaspoons butter	2 teaspoons minced parsley
2 teaspoons finely chopped onion	Freshly ground black pepper
2 tablespoons dry white wine	to taste

1. Cut the fillet into 2 strips.
2. Roll each strip and secure with a toothpick.
3. Heat the butter in a skillet and sauté and stir the onion until it is translucent, just a minute or so.

4. Place the fillet rolls in the skillet and pour the wine over them. Add the tomatoes and parsley and bring to a boil. Reduce the heat and cook over a low flame for 10 to 12 minutes, or until the fish flakes at the touch of a fork. Turn several times during the cooking.
5. Remove the cooked fillet rolls to a warm serving platter and keep warm.
6. Stir the sauce remaining in the skillet over medium-high heat and pour it over the fish. Season with pepper and serve immediately.

BLACKOUT PUDDING

1 tablespoon butter plus butter for the baking dish	⅓ cup grated Gruyere cheese
1 ear of corn	1 teaspoon cornstarch
1 3¾-ounce can salmon	2 teaspoons water
1 tablespoon flour	1 egg yolk
½ cup milk	Pinch of crushed red pepper flakes
Salt and freshly ground black pepper	Pinch of nutmeg

1. Heat the oven to 375 degrees.
2. Butter a small ovenproof dish.
3. Cut the kernels from the cob of corn and flake the salmon.
4. Melt 1 tablespoon butter in a small saucepan and stir in the flour. Cook for 1 minute and add the milk, stirring vigorously, until it begins to thicken. Season with salt and pepper to taste. Add the corn, stir; add the salmon, then the cheese. Mix well after each addition.
5. Mix the cornstarch and water in a cup and add it to the pudding. Add the egg yolk and stir again. Season with crushed red pepper and nutmeg. Pour the mixture into the prepared dish.
6. Bake for 25 minutes and serve hot.

SALMON AND MASHED POTATOES

3 teaspoons butter	1 teaspoon lemon juice
2 teaspoons flour	1 3¾-ounce can salmon
½ cup milk	2 small potatoes, peeled and
Salt	sliced

1. Melt 2 teaspoon butter in a small casserole and stir in the flour. Cook, stirring for 1 minute and pour in the milk all at once, stirring vigorously. Continue stirring until the sauce begins to thicken.
2. Add salt to taste and lemon juice and continue stirring. Now add the salmon and mix well. Set aside.
3. Prepare mashed potatoes: Cover the potatoes with salted water. Cook for 20 minutes, or until tender. Purée the potatoes and stir in salt to taste and 1 teaspoon butter. Set aside.
4. At dinnertime warm up the salmon and taste for seasonings. Present the mashed potatoes in a ring on a warm serving plate and top with the salmon.

POACHED SALMON

2 slices carrot	1 tablespoon vinegar
1 slice onion	1 sprig parsley
½ stalk celery, sliced	2 cups water
1 teaspoon butter	Salt to taste
2 peppercorns	1 slice (about ½ pound with
1 clove	bone) fresh salmon

1. Sauté the carrot, onion, and celery in butter, stirring, for 1 or 2 minutes. Add the peppercorns, clove, vinegar, parsley, water, and salt to taste. Bring to a boil.
2. Put the salmon in the boiling court bouillon and let it simmer for 8 minutes. Turn once. Let the salmon cool in the liquid. Serve hot with butter and lemon. Serve cold with mayonnaise, or such sauces as cucumber sauce.

BROILED SALMON STEAK WITH DILL

1 tablespoon vegetable oil	2 teaspoons melted butter
1 tablespoon finely chopped dill	Parsley for garnish
Salt and freshly ground black	Lemon wedges
pepper	
½ pound slice fresh salmon	

1. Mix the oil with dill and salt and pepper to taste in a dish and add the salmon. Coat the salmon on both sides and let the fish marinate for ½ hour. Turn the fish occasionally.
2. Preheat the broiler to high.
3. Broil the salmon for 3 minutes on each side. Brush with butter, garnish with parsley, and serve with lemon wedges.

SALMON AND CORN CASSEROLE

1 tablespoon butter plus enough to grease the casserole	¼ cup chopped green pepper
1 small onion, peeled and chopped	Salt and freshly ground black pepper
1 tablespoon flour	1 3¾-ounce can salmon
½ cup milk	1 slice white bread, trimmed and crumbled
1 ear of fresh corn	

1. Melt the butter in a saucepan and add the chopped onion. Cook, stirring for 1 minute. Mix in the flour and pour in the milk. Stir until the sauce begins to thicken.
2. Cut the kernels of corn off the cob and add them to the sauce. Add the diced green pepper and salt and pepper to taste.
3. Flake the salmon and stir it into the seasoned corn mixture.
4. Preheat the oven to 350 degrees.
5. Pour the salmon and corn mixture into a buttered baking dish and top with the bread crumbs. Cover with foil and bake for 30 minutes. Put under the broiler until the crumbs are well browned.

Note: Cream-style canned corn may be substituted for fresh corn.

SALMON PUDDING

1 slice trimmed white bread
2 stalks celery, trimmed, washed, and cut into 1-inch pieces
1 3¾-ounce can salmon, drained
1 egg
  Salt and freshly ground black pepper

1 teaspoon lemon juice
1 teaspoon sugar
1 teaspoon sweet India relish
  Lemon wedges (optional)
  Mushroom Sauce, see recipe page 211 (optional)

1. Crumble the bread in a food processor or blender and set it aside.
2. Put the celery in the container of a food processor or blender and chop it coarsely. Add the bread crumbs, salmon, egg, salt and pepper to taste, lemon juice, sugar, and India relish. Turn the motor on for a second and then turn it off. Scrape down the sides of the container with a small spatula, and turn the motor on again for a second.
3. Preheat the oven to 350 degrees.
4. Butter an ovenproof baking dish and add the salmon mixture to it. Bake for 30 minutes. Serve with lemon wedges or Mushroom Sauce.

Note: If you don't have a food processor or blender, crumble the bread by hand and chop the celery very fine. Flake the drained salmon and put it in a mixing bowl. Add the bread and the remaining ingredients and mix well.

POACHED SHAD ROE

1 pair shad roe
1 tablespoon flour
⅔ stick butter

  Salt and freshly ground black pepper
  Parsley for garnish
  Juice of ½ lemon

1. Wash the roe in cold water and separate the pair by cutting away the membrane which joins them. Discard it. Dry the roe on paper towels and keep them cool until cooking time.

2. Spread the flour on a sheet of wax paper and roll the roe in the flour to coat both sides.
3. Melt the butter in a heavy skillet with a cover.
4. Place the floured roe in the skillet and turn to coat both sides with the melted butter. Reduce the heat to low and cover the skillet. Cook for 10 minutes and turn the roe. Continue cooking, still covered, for another 10 minutes.
5. Sprinkle the cooked roe with salt and pepper to taste, parsley, and lemon juice. Serve on a warm plate with some of the hot butter sauce. Don't pour all of it over the roe; it is too much. Don't be afraid to add more lemon juice as you dine.

Note: Crisp bacon goes well with this dish.

TUNA BAKE ITALIAN-STYLE

2 ounces pasta, spaghetti, or macaroni, cooked al dente according to package directions
1 3¼-ounce can chunk-style tuna
1 8-ounce can tomato sauce or stewed tomatoes
¼ grated Parmesan cheese
1 teaspoon chopped parsley

1 small onion, peeled and chopped
1 stalk of celery, trimmed, washed, and minced
1 teaspoon dried oregano
Salt and freshly ground black pepper
Olive oil to grease the casserole

1. Prepare the oven to 350 degrees.
2. Combine the pasta, tuna, tomato sauce, cheese, parsley, onion, celery, and oregano, with salt and pepper to taste. Blend well.
3. Oil a small casserole and add the fish mixture. Cover with foil.
4. Bake for 30 minutes. Remove the cover and continue baking for another 15 minutes. Serve hot with additional cheese, if desired.

TUNA DELIGHT

1 or 2 small potatoes	¼ teaspoon Worcestershire sauce
1 or 2 small carrots	1 3½-ounce can of tuna
1 tablespoon plus 3 teaspoons butter	2 tablespoons dehydrated mushroom slices
1 tablespoon flour	1 tablespoon sliced pimiento
½ cup milk	1 tablespoon chopped onion
Salt and freshly ground black pepper	

1. Peel and pare the potato and carrot and slice them in thin slices. Put them in a small saucepan and cover with water. Add salt to taste and bring to a boil. Reduce the heat and cook until tender, about 20 minutes. Purée the vegetables in a food mill, food processor, or blender and season with 2 teaspoons of butter and salt and pepper to taste. Blend well.
2. Put 1 tablespoon of butter in a saucepan over low heat and add the flour. Stir and add the milk, stirring constantly, until the sauce thickens. Season with Worcestershire sauce and salt and pepper to taste. Then stir in the tuna, mushrooms, pimiento, and onion. Blend well and cook for a minute or so.
3. Butter a flameproof casserole with 1 teaspoon butter and pour in the creamed tuna. Cover the tuna with the potato and carrot purée. Put under the broiler for about 3 minutes, or until well browned.

RISOTTO WITH CLAMS

2 teaspoons olive oil	1 teaspoon basil
2 tablespoons chopped shallots	Pinch of saffron
1 clove garlic, peeled and minced	1 6½-ounce can minced clams
1 small tomato, peeled, cored, seeded, and diced	2 tablespoons dry rice
2 tablespoons chopped parsley	Salt

1. Heat the oil in a small heavy pot with a cover and sauté the shallots and garlic until translucent, about 3 minutes.
2. Add the tomato pulp, the juice from the can of clams, the parsley, basil, and saffron. Bring to a boil, stir, and simmer for 10 minutes.
3. Add the diced clams, rice, and salt to taste and mix well. Cover the pot and simmer for 20 minutes, or until the rice is cooked. Serve hot.

CREAMED MINCED CLAMS

2 teaspoons butter	1 tablespoon dry white wine
1 6½-ounce can minced clams	Salt and freshly ground black
1 tablespoon chopped shallots	pepper
2 tablespoons dried mushrooms	1 tablespoon cream
2 tablespoons chopped tomatoes or 4 cherry tomatoes in halves	1 tablespoon chopped parsley

1. Heat the butter in a skillet and add the drained clams. Cook, stirring, for 2 minutes. Remove the clams and keep them warm.
2. Add a bit more butter, if necessary, to the skillet and sauté the shallots for 1 minute and add the mushrooms. Stir and add the tomatoes. Stir and add the wine. Cook to reduce the liquid to almost nothing.
3. Season with salt and pepper to taste and stir in the cream. Test the seasonings and adjust to your taste. Serve hot with rice and sprinkle with parsley.

Note: As you might guess, this is better with fresh clams and fresh mushrooms. But this is for the day you missed shopping and have canned clams and dried mushrooms in the pantry.

CLAMS IN WINE SAUCE

8 Littleneck clams or ¼ to ½ cup canned minced clams
2 teaspoons butter
1 tablespoon finely minced shallots
2 teaspoons flour
⅛ teaspoon Worcestershire sauce

2 drops Tabasco
¼ cup dry white wine
Salt and freshly ground black pepper
¼ teaspoon Pernod or other anise-flavored liquor

1. Open the clams with a strong knife and scrape out the clams and catch the juice. Alternatively, measure out ¼ to ½ cup canned minced clams. Catch the liquid from the can and reserve it.
2. Melt the butter in a skillet and stir in the minced shallots. Cook for a minute, or until they are wilted.
3. Sprinkle the shallots with flour and stir to blend well. Stir constantly and pour in the clam liquid and the wine. There should be a total of ½ cup liquid. In case there is not enough clam liquid, add wine to make the measure.
4. Season the sauce with Worcestershire sauce, Tabasco, and salt and pepper to taste. Mix well. Stir in the Pernod.
5. Keep the fire low throughout the cooking and finally add the clams and stir to mix well with the sauce. Just heat through and serve. Do not let the clams and sauce boil. Serve on toast or with rice.

OYSTER FRITTERS

6 oysters	2 tablespoons vegetable oil
1 egg	Salt
1 tablespoon water	Cayenne pepper
2 slices trimmed white bread in crumbs	Lemon wedges

1. Drain and rinse the oysters. Dry them on paper towels.
2. Beat together the egg and water.
3. Dip the oysters in the egg and water mixture and then in the bread crumbs. Repeat until a good coating is formed.
4. Heat the oil to quite hot and sauté the oysters for 1 or 2 minutes on each side. Shake the pan and keep the oysters from burning. Remove the sauteed oysters and cover to keep warm.
5. Season the oysters with salt and cayenne pepper to taste and serve hot with lemon wedges.

STUFFED CRAB

3 tablespoons butter	¼ pound shredded crabmeat
2 scallions, trimmed and chopped, including green tops	1 teaspoon curry powder
½ clove garlic, peeled and minced	1 teaspoon chopped parsley
Crushed red pepper flakes	Fresh coriander to taste (optional)
1 slice white bread, trimmed, in crumbs	Salt to taste
	Lime or lemon wedges

1. Preheat the oven to 400 degrees.
2. Melt the butter in a skillet and sauté the chopped scallions and garlic. Season with crushed red pepper flakes to taste. Stir and cook for 1 minute.
3. Add the bread crumbs, crabmeat, curry powder, parsley, coriander, if desired, and salt to taste and mix well. Spoon into ramekins or shells.
4. Bake for 15 minutes and serve with lime or lemon wedges.

CREAMED CRAB ON HAM AND TOAST

1 ounce country-cured or other ham in a thin slice	¼ cup light cream
1 teaspoon butter	¼ teaspoon Worcestershire sauce
1 tablespoon chopped shallots	¼ pound fresh crabmeat
1 tablespoon dry sherry	1 slice white bread, trimmed and toasted

1. In a skillet, sauté the ham over very low heat for 4 minutes on each side. Remove and keep it warm.
2. Melt the butter in the skillet and sauté the chopped shallots over medium heat until wilted. Stir to keep from scorching.
3. Add the sherry and cook to reduce by half.
4. Stir in the cream and cook down a bit over fairly high heat for about 2 minutes. Season with Worcestershire sauce.
5. Add the crab and mix well. Set aside until serving time.
6. At serving time put the toast on a warm plate and top it with the cooked ham. Pour the creamed crab over and serve immediately.

CRABMEAT MORNAY

1 teaspoon butter	½ teaspoon Worcestershire sauce
1 teaspoon flour	Salt
½ cup milk	¼ pound crabmeat, flaked
¼ cup grated Cheddar or Gruyere cheese	2 teaspoons lemon juice
½ teaspoon prepared mustard	1 slice trimmed white bread in crumbs

1. Preheat the oven to 400 degrees.
2. Melt the butter in a small saucepan and add the flour and stir to blend well.
3. Pour in the milk and continue stirring. Add the cheese, mustard, Worcestershire sauce, and salt to taste. Blend well.
4. Arrange the crabmeat in an ovenproof dish. Sprinkle with lemon juice and bread crumbs. Add cheese sauce and butter.
5. Bake for 12 minutes, or until golden.

BOILED LOBSTER

1   1½-pound live lobster   1   tablespoon salt per quart of
    Water to cover   water

1. Bring the salted water to a rapid boil and put the live lobster
   head first into the boiling water. Cover and cook for 20 to 25
   minutes. Reduce the heat if the pot tends to boil over.
2. Drain the boiled lobster and pour cold water over it to stop the
   cooking. Let the lobster cool.
3. Break the claws off the body and crack them with a nut or
   lobster cracker or mallet. Remove the claw meat.
4. Separate the tail from the body of the lobster and remove the
   fins from the end of the tail. Slide out the tail meat. Cut through
   the center of the tail meat to reveal the intestinal tract. Remove
   and discard it.
5. Pick out the body meat and discard the stomach and liver
   (the sack at the head end of the body near the head). Pick out
   any meat available in the remaining body and feelers.
6. Serve the lobster meat with melted hot butter or cool the meat
   and serve it with mayonnaise.

BAKED LOBSTER

1   1½-pound live lobster   2   tablespoons butter, melted
    Salt and freshly ground black 1   teaspoon olive oil
    pepper   Juice of 1 lemon

1. Preheat the oven to 325 degrees.
2. Place the lobster on its back on a flat steady surface. Plunge a
   heavy kitchen knife into the center of the lobster where the tail
   and body meet to kill the lobster quickly.
3. Cut the lobster down the center into halves. Discard the tough
   sac near the eyes. Retain the red and green liver and coral.

4. Season the lobster meat with salt and pepper to taste. Dribble the olive oil onto the flesh and squeeze over all the juice of half a lemon.
5. Place the lobster in a baking pan and bake for 15 minutes.
6. Baste with butter and bake for another 15 minutes.
7. Serve immediately with any remaining butter and lemon.

CREAMED SCALLOPS AND MUSHROOMS

1 tablespoon butter	½ cup sliced mushrooms or about
¼ pound scallops	¼ cup dehydrated mushrooms
Salt and freshly ground black	4 cherry tomatoes, halved
pepper	1 tablespoon dry white wine
2 teaspoons chopped shallots	2 tablespoons cream
	1 teaspoon chopped parsley

1. Heat the butter in a skillet large enough to hold all the scallops without crowding.
2. When the butter is quite hot, but not browning, add the scallops and stir and shake the pan to prevent sticking and to brown the scallops on all sides. Cook for 1 or 2 minutes or until golden or light gold. Do not overcook. Salt and pepper the scallops to taste.
3. Remove the scallops with a slotted spoon and keep them warm.
4. Add the chopped shallots to the skillet and cook briefly, stirring continuously. Then add the mushrooms and cherry tomatoes and stir again. Cook for about 1 minute and add the wine and cook to reduce to half.
5. Add the cream and stir to blend well. Cook over high heat about 1 minute, stirring and scraping the sides and bottom of the skillet. Add the scallops and blend well. Test for seasoning and add more salt, if necessary. Serve hot garnished with parsley, if desired.

SHRIMP CAPRICE

2 tablespoons butter
½ cup shelled and washed fresh peas
¼ teaspoon sugar
Salt and freshly ground black pepper to taste

1 tablespoon chopped shallots
5 shrimp, shelled and deveined
½ teaspoon flour
2 tablespoons heavy cream

1. Melt 1 tablespoon of the butter in a small pot with a cover. Add peas, cover, and simmer over low heat for 20 minutes.
2. Season the peas with sugar and salt and pepper to taste.
3. Melt the remaining butter in a small skillet and add the chopped shallots. Stir and cook until wilted. Add the shrimp and stir and cook for 3 minutes.
4. Sprinkle the shrimp with the flour and stir to distribute it well.
5. Combine the peas with the shrimp and mix well. Add the cream and cook, stirring, for 2 minutes. Serve immediately.

CURRIED SCALLOPS

1 tablespoon butter
¼ teaspoon cumin
¼ teaspoon turmeric
⅛ teaspoon ground coriander
¼ teaspoon salt

1 tablespoon lemon juice
¼ pound bay scallops (ocean scallops may be used cut in quarters or finer, but the dish will not be as good)

1. Melt the butter in a skillet over low heat and add the seasonings. Simmer the sauce, stirring, for 1 minute, or until the ingredients are incorporated and bubbling.
2. Heat the broiler to hot.
3. Arrange the scallops in a baking dish in one layer and pour the sauce over them. Lift and turn the scallops in the sauce to coat all sides.
4. Broil for 5 minutes, or until the scallops are golden and the sauce is bubbling.

SCALLOPS WITH LEEK

4 teaspoons butter
1 small leek, trimmed, washed, and chopped
Salt and freshly ground black pepper
2 teaspoons dry white wine
2 teaspoons light cream

2 teaspoons finely chopped shallots
¼ pound bay scallops or sea scallops in quarters
1 teaspoon Pernod or Ricard or other anise-flavored liqueur

1. Heat 2 teaspoons of the butter in a small saucepan and cook the chopped leek for 1 minute. Add salt and pepper to taste.
2. Add the wine and cook, stirring, for 1 minute. Add the cream and simmer, stirring, for about 7 to 8 minutes. Don't let the chopped leek burn.
3. In a separate skillet melt the remaining 2 teaspoons of butter and add the shallots. Cook over low heat, stirring for about 1 minute. Season again with salt and pepper and add the scallops. Stir and add the Pernod. Mix again and bring to full heat for 1 minute. Mix the two batches and combine well. Serve hot.

CHINESE-STYLE STIR-FRIED SHRIMP

8 medium-sized shrimp
1 teaspoon cornstarch
1 tablespoon light soy sauce
1 teaspoon sugar
1 tablespoon vinegar
Salt

1 clove garlic, peeled and finely minced
2 tablespoons chopped scallions
2 tablespoons finely chopped fresh ginger
¼ cup vegetable oil

1. Shell and devein the shrimp and pat them dry with paper towels. Place them in a small mixing bowl and add the cornstarch. Turn the shrimp until they are all coated with cornstarch.
2. In another bowl combine the soy sauce, sugar, and vinegar, with salt to taste.
3. In a third bowl, mix the garlic, scallions, and ginger.

4. Heat the oil in a wok or frying pan and when it is hot add the shrimp. Stir and cook for 1½ to 2 minutes. Drain the shrimp in a sieve and retain the cooking oil.
5. Return 2 teaspoons of the cooking oil to the wok and discard the remainder. Heat the oil and add the ginger mixture to it. Stir and add the vinegar mixture. When it boils add the shrimp and blend well. Serve with rice.

ITALIAN-STYLE BAKED SHRIMP

6 medium-sized raw shrimp	Salt and freshly ground black
2 tablespoons chopped onions	pepper to taste
1 small tomato, cored, peeled,	1 teaspoon oregano
and diced	2 teaspoons olive oil
1 teaspoon Italian parsley	1 slice white bread, trimmed

1. Shell and devein the shrimp. Set the shrimp aside and retain the shells.
2. Place the shrimp shells in a small saucepan. Cover them with water and add a little salt. Bring to a boil and simmer for 20 minutes. Let the shells cool in the water and discard them. Place the shrimp water over heat and reduce it to about 3 tablespoons.
3. In a skillet, sauté the onion in the olive oil for about 2 minutes. Add the diced tomato, oregano, salt and pepper, and parsley. Mix well. Cook a few minutes. Add the reduced shrimp water.
4. Preheat the oven to 350 degrees.
5. Place the shrimp in an ovenproof casserole and pour the sauce over them.
6. Roughly crumble the slice of bread and add the crumbs to the casserole.
7. Bake for 20 minutes. Then put under the broiler for 2 or 3 minutes, or until the crumbs are browned well. Serve hot.

SHRIMP WITH CAPERS AND DILL

¼ pound shrimp
Salt and freshly ground black
pepper
1 tablespoon butter

2 teaspoons lemon juice
2 teaspoons capers
1 teaspoon chopped fresh dill
2 teaspoons Cognac (optional)

1. Peel and devein the shrimp. Sprinkle with salt and pepper.
2. Heat the butter in a small skillet and, when it is hot, add the shrimp. Cook for 4 minutes, stirring frequently.
3. Add the lemon juice, capers, dill, and salt and pepper to taste.
4. Warm the Cognac just before pouring it over the shrimp and ignite it. Serve immediately.

SHRIMP NEWBURG

2 teaspoons butter
8 medium shrimp, shelled and
deveined
½ teaspoon paprika
Salt and freshly ground black
pepper

1 tablespoon finely chopped
shallots
¼ cup plus 1 tablespoon cream
1 tablespoon dry sherry
1 egg yolk

1. Melt the butter in a heavy skillet and add the shrimp. Shake the skillet and cook briefly. Season the shrimp with paprika and salt and pepper to taste.
2. Sprinkle the chopped shallots over the shrimp. Add the sherry and mix well. Continue stirring until the shrimp have lost their raw look and turn pink. Remove the shrimp and keep them warm.
3. Reduce any pan liquid to almost nothing and add the ¼ cup cream. Cook for 1 minute over medium-high heat.
4. Mix the egg yolk and the 1 tablespoon of cream together. Remove the skillet from the heat and stir in the egg yolk and cream mixture. Warm the sauce well but gently and add the shrimp. Do not boil. Serve with rice or a scalloped vegetable.

Rice and Other Accompaniments

The enjoyment of richly seasoned foods is always increased by the company of a subtle foil such as Simple Rice, Rice and Peas, Polenta, or Yorkshire Pudding. It's deplorable, but I have observed many people who, under the curse of dieting, have refrained from partaking of bread, rice, or potatoes that would have been so good with the rich sauce at hand. I have also observed lovers of good food use rice or bread to sop up that aromatic sauce until the plate is clean. That's what I like to see!

RICE WITH GREEN PEPPER AND TOMATO PUREE

1 medium-sized green pepper, cut into 1-inch cubes	2 tablespoons water
1 small onion, peeled and chopped	1 teaspoon sugar
¼ cup tomato purée	Salt and freshly ground black pepper to taste
	2 tablespoons raw rice

1. Put all ingredients in a small heavy saucepan with a cover. Bring to a boil, lower the heat, and simmer for ½ hour, or until the rice is tender. Taste and correct the seasonings, if necessary.

SIMPLE RICE

This is a perfect accompaniment for sauced dishes.

2 tablespoons water
2 tablespoons rice

Salt to taste

1. Bring the water to boil in a small heavy pot with a cover. Stir in the rice and salt.
2. Cover the pot, lower the heat, and cook for about 9 minutes, or until the water is absorbed. Use a Flame-Tamer to maintain the low heat.

RICE AND PEAS

2 teaspoons butter
1 teaspoon chopped onion
2 tablespoons raw rice
4 tablespoons water
¼ bay leaf

Dash of Tabasco
Salt and freshly ground black pepper
½ cup hulled fresh peas
¼ cup chicken broth

1. Melt the butter in a small heavy pot with tight-fitting cover. Add the onion, and sauté until wilted, 1 or 2 minutes. Stir in the rice, water, bay leaf, Tabasco, and salt and pepper to taste. Cover tightly and cook over the lowest heat possible, for 10 minutes, or until the rice is almost tender.
2. Put the peas in a saucepan and cover with the broth. Add a little salt and pepper and bring to a boil. Cover and cook over very low heat until the peas are tender.
3. When cooked, combine the peas and rice. Taste and correct the seasonings, if necessary. Serve hot.

LOUISIANA RICE

1 medium-sized green pepper, cut into 1-inch pieces
1 small tomato, cored, washed, and sliced
1 small onion, peeled and thinly sliced

1 tablespoon dry rice
¼ cup water
Salt and crushed red pepper flakes to taste

Combine all ingredients in a small heavy pot with a cover. Cover tightly and cook, over the lowest heat possible, until the rice is al dente.

YORKSHIRE PUDDING

¼ cup flour
2 tablespoons milk
Salt to taste

A few drops olive or vegetable oil
1 egg

1. Mix the flour, milk, salt, oil, and egg into a paste, beating to incorporate as much air into the mixture as possible.
2. Let the batter stand for 1 hour.
3. Preheat the oven to 350 degrees.
4. Line a pie pan with aluminum foil. Spread a few drops of oil over the aluminum foil. If you are cooking roast beef to serve with the pudding, use a few drops of beef dripping instead of oil.
5. Place the oiled foil and pan in the oven and let it get hot. Pour in the batter and let it bake 40 minutes. Serve with roast beef, oven-barbecued chicken, or any other robust meat.

POLENTA

¼ cup yellow cornmeal   ½ teaspoon salt
2 cups water

1. Combine all ingredients in a saucepan and cook over medium heat, stirring constantly, for 10 minutes. Set aside.
2. At serving time heat the polenta and continue stirring for another 5 minutes. Serve hot with butter or parmesan cheese or both, or cover with a favorite spaghetti sauce.

DRESSING FOR POULTRY

1 13-ounce can chicken broth
Butter
4 or 5 slices of day-old white bread, trimmed
Salt and freshly ground black pepper
2 small carrots, trimmed, scraped, washed, and chopped

1 hard-cooked egg, diced
2 stalks celery, trimmed, washed, and finely chopped
2 small onions, peeled and chopped
¼ cup diced green pepper

1. Preheat the oven to 300 degrees.
2. Combine the chicken broth with 1 chopped onion, 1 chopped carrot, 1 stalk celery, chopped, and salt and pepper to taste in a small saucepan. Simmer for 2 hours. Strain and discard the solids. Any excess can be used to make gravy for the poultry.
3. Butter a baking dish with a cover.
4. Mix together the bread, egg, and the remaining celery, onion, green pepper, and carrot. Moisten with the strained chicken broth. Season with salt and pepper. Spoon into the prepared baking dish.
5. Bake, covered, for 1 hour. Remove the cover during the last half hour or so if you like crust on your dressing.

CORN FRITTERS WITH HOT PEPPERS

The recipe makes 10 or so small fritters or 2 large ones

⅓ cup cream-style corn
1 egg, separated
1 tablespoon flour
1 tablespoon cornmeal
Salt and freshly ground black
pepper to taste

1 tablespoon milk
2 teaspoons finely minced hot
cherry peppers
Butter

1. Pour the creamed corn into a small bowl and add the egg yolk, flour, cornmeal, salt, and pepper. Stir well and add the minced hot peppers and milk. Blend well.
2. Beat the egg white stiff and fold it in.
3. Melt a little butter in a small skillet or griddle and coat the bottom over low heat. Spoon several separate tablespoons of batter in to make several small fritters. Brown on both sides and serve hot.

SAGE DUMPLINGS

2 tablespoons flour
½ teaspoon baking powder
Pinch of salt

Pinch of sage
½ teaspoon shortening
1 tablespoon milk

1. Sift the flour, baking powder, and salt into a small bowl. Crush the sage between your fingers and add it to the bowl.
2. Cut in the shortening, using a knife or spatula, until the mixture resembles coarse meal. Stir in the milk until a ball of dough forms. Set aside for a few minutes.
3. Drop the dough by spoonfuls into the simmering liquid. Cook uncovered for 3 minutes. Cover, and cook for 10 minutes longer.

Vegetables

Vegetables speak for themselves with their fresh-from-the-garden variety of flavors and colors blessed by the sun, earth, and moisture. I seldom use frozen or canned vegetables. I can find just the quantity I need for one serving in the local markets which sell fresh-grown vegetables. But, if necessary, there is no problem in using a portion of a small supermarket package and refrigerating the remainder or using it in soups and stews. Just hunt for fresh, bright, crisp produce, and cook it to your taste. But remember, whether you are preparing a Corn, Zucchini, and Cheese Casserole, Italian Green Beans, or Yellow Squash in Sauce Ann, be sure to let the intrinsic flavor of the vegetables predominate and allow some texture and bite to remain in the dish—don't overseason or overcook!

ARTICHOKE BOTTOM

1 artichoke	Salt to taste
Water to cover	

1. Cut off the stem of the artichoke flush with the bottom. Discard the stem. Slice off the top of the artichoke, leaving 1 or 1½ inches of bottom, depending on the size of the vegetable.
2. Peel off the green leaves around the bottom of the artichoke and pare the artichoke bottom down to the white layers with a sharp knife. Immediately rub the white with cut of lemon to impede darkening. Leave some of the green leaves and the choke in until after cooking.

3. Place the trimmed artichoke in a small pot with a cover. Cover the artichoke with water. Add salt to taste and bring to a boil on top of the stove. Reduce the heat and simmer, covered, for 20 minutes. Let the artichoke cool in the liquid in which it was cooked.

4. Using a small spoon, scoop out the inedible, prickly choke and refrigerate until serving time. The artichoke bottom can be served hot by sautéeing it in a little butter and then topping it with a little tomato sauce, hollandaise sauce, or a sprinkling of fresh lemon juice. To serve the artichoke bottom cold, slice it and add it to your favorite salad or dress it with mayonnaise, lemon juice, or your favorite salad dressing.

BRAISED ARTICHOKE

1 artichoke	1 small tomato, peeled, cored, and diced
Lemon juice	
1 small onion, peeled and chopped	Salt and freshly ground black pepper
1 clove garlic, peeled and mashed	1 cup of chicken broth
1 small carrot, trimmed, scraped, washed, and chopped	Butter or vinaigrette dressing (optional)

1. Cut the top and the stem off the artichoke and trim off the pointed tops of the leaves.
2. Slice the artichoke in half and remove the fibrous choke at the bottom of the artichoke along with some of the purplish inner leaves above the choke to make a stuffable cavity.
3. Rub the cut surfaces with lemon juice.
4. Place the artichoke halves in an ovenproof casserole with a cover. Add the vegetables and add salt and pepper to taste.
5. Preheat oven to 350 degrees.
6. Pour the chicken broth over the vegetables. Cover it and bake for 50 minutes.
7. Serve the vegetable hot with butter or cold with vinaigrette dressing.

STUFFED ARTICHOKE

1 artichoke
½ slice trimmed white bread in crumbs
2 tablespoons chopped celery
Salt and freshly ground black pepper

1 small onion, peeled and finely chopped
Butter
Water

1. Trim the stem off the bottom of the artichoke and cut off an inch or so of the top of the artichoke. Then cut off the top point of each leaf.
2. Wash the artichoke well under cold running water. Drain well.
3. Place the artichoke on a flat surface and using both hands coax the petals away from the center of the vegetable and open up a stuffable center. Before stuffing remove the choke from the bottom of the opening. Use a sharp knife to cut around the choke and dig it out with a spoon or a melon ball cutter. Remove all the choke so that the artichoke bottom is revealed.
4. Blend together the bread crumbs, onion, and celery with salt and pepper to taste. Stuff the cavity and the spaces between the leaves. Top with a pat of butter and place in an ovenproof casserole with a cover. Use aluminum foil to hold the artichoke upright if necessary. Add a little water to the pan.
5. Preheat the oven to 350 degrees.
6. Bake covered tightly for 1 hour.

ASPARAGUS DINNER

12 medium-sized asparagus spears
Salt to taste
1 tablespoon butter
1 tablespoon flour
1 cup milk

¼ teaspoon Worcestershire sauce
½ cup grated Gruyere, Swiss, or Cheddar cheese
1 hard-cooked egg

1. Peel the asparagus spears with a potato peeler and cut off the bottom tough part of each spear. Discard the bottom parts or save them for asparagus soup.

2. Cover the asparagus with water and add a little salt. Bring them to a boil and simmer for about 7 minutes, or until they are tender to the touch of a fork. Drain and keep warm.
3. Melt the butter in a small saucepan and stir in the flour. Cook for a few seconds and pour in the milk all at once, stirring vigorously. When the sauce begins to thicken, add the Worcestershire sauce and grated cheese and continue stirring until the the sauce is smooth.
4. Slice or dice the hard-cooked egg.
5. Arrange the drained, cooked asparagus on a warm plate and cover with the cheese sauce. Sprinkle the dish with diced or sliced egg. Add a little more sauce and serve hot.

Note: Any leftover sauce can be served on toast for breakfast.

BRAISED ASPARAGUS

6 or more spears asparagus, depending on size	Salt and freshly ground black pepper
1 tablespoon butter	1 tablespoon lemon juice
	¼ teaspoon sugar

1. Peel the spears of asparagus and cut off and discard the tough bottom of each stalk. Place the spears flat on the cutting board or whatever space you use and cut the stalks on the diagonal into 1-inch lengths.
2. Melt the butter in a skillet with a cover or a small casserole. Add salt and pepper to taste, lemon juice, and sugar. Over medium heat cook the asparagus, stirring continuously, for 2 minutes.
3. Cover the asparagus and cook over low heat for about 5 minutes. Test for doneness. Uncover and turn up the heat and cook, stirring, for another minute to brown the asparagus slightly.

ASPARAGUS WITH LEMON-CHEESE SAUCE

6 asparagus spears
2 teaspoons melted butter
2 teaspoons lemon juice

Salt to taste
2 teaspoons grated Parmesan
cheese

1. Cook the asparagus until tender in water to cover. Drain and keep warm.
2. Mix the butter, lemon juice, salt, and cheese in a small cup.
3. Serve the asparagus on a warm plate with the sauce.

BROCCOLI IN VINEGAR SAUCE

2 slices bacon
¼ cup diced onion
¼ cup vinegar
1 tablespoon sugar

1 cup broccoli flowerettes
Salt and freshly ground black
pepper

1. Wash and trim the broccoli flowerettes and put them in a saucepan with water to cover and salt to taste. Bring to a boil and simmer, partially covered for 5 minutes. Drain and set aside.
2. In a skillet cook the bacon over low heat until crisp, adding the diced onion toward the last of the cooking. When the bacon is crisp and rendered of its fat, drain in a sieve to remove the excess fat. Cut the bacon into small dice. Wipe out the skillet and return the bacon-onion mixture to the skillet. Over low heat add the vinegar and sugar and stir well.
3. Put the drained broccoli into the saucepan and pour the sauce over it. Stir well and heat through. Serve with freshly ground black pepper.

BROCCOLI MORNAY

1 cup broccoli flowerettes	½ cup milk
Salt and freshly ground black pepper	½ cup grated Cheddar cheese
	Worcestershire sauce to taste
1 teaspoon flour	Tabasco sauce to taste
1 teaspoon butter	

1. Put the broccoli in a saucepan with water to cover and salt to taste. Bring to a boil and simmer for about 4 minutes. Do not overcook. Drain and set aside.
2. In another saucepan melt the butter and stir in the flour. Cook very briefly and stir in the milk. Stir with a wire whisk until the sauce begins to thicken. Swirl in the cheese and stir until it is incorporated. Season with Worcestershire and Tabasco sauce.
3. Put the broccoli in a small casserole without a top. Pour the cheese sauce over the broccoli and season with salt and pepper to taste. Put under the broiler at low heat until the cheese is bubbling. Serve hot.

BRUSSELS SPROUTS WITH WILTED ONION

4 ounces (5 or 6) brussels sprouts, washed	2 teaspoons butter
	1 tablespoon chopped onion
Salt to taste	

1. Trim off the ends and damaged outer leaves of the sprouts. Put them in a saucepan with water to cover and salt to taste. Bring to a boil and simmer for 10 minutes. Drain and set aside.
2. Heat the butter in a saucepan and cook the chopped onion until it is translucent or wilted. Add the sprouts, cover, and simmer for another 5 minutes. Serve hot.

FRIED CABBAGE

1 cup shredded cabbage	Salt and freshly ground black
1 tablespoon chopped onion	pepper
1 slice bacon	Pinch of paprika
	1 tablespoon sour cream or cream

1. In a skillet, cook the bacon until it is crisp. Set it aside to drain on paper towels.
2. In 1 teaspoon of the rendered bacon fat sauté the onion and add the cabbage. Cook until tender, about 6 minutes or so.
3. Season with salt and pepper to taste, paprika, and sour cream and heat through. Crumble the bacon and sprinkle it on top of the cabbage and serve.

VEGETABLE PUREE

¼ head of a medium-sized cabbage, finely chopped	2 small tomatoes, cored and chopped
1 medium-sized onion, peeled and chopped	Salt and freshly ground black pepper to taste
	2 teaspoons butter

1. Put all ingredients in a saucepan with a tight-fitting cover. Put the pan over the lowest flame possible and cook until the vegetables are tender.
2. Purée the cooked vegetables in a food mill, food processor, or blender. Test for seasonings and add more salt or butter, if necessary. Serve hot.

CARROT PUDDING

2 carrots, trimmed, scraped, washed, and sliced	Salt and freshly ground black pepper
1 egg yolk	1 tablespoon cream
	1 teaspoon butter, melted

1. Put the carrots in saucepan with salted water and boil until tender. Purée the carrots in a food mill, food processor, or blender.
2. Sprinkle the puréed carrots with salt and pepper to taste and add the egg yolk and cream. Mix well.
3. Preheat the oven to 350 degrees.
4. Use some of the melted butter to grease the inside of a small Pyrex cup. Pour the rest of the butter into the carrot purée and mix well. Then turn the mixture into the greased cup.
5. Bake for 1 hour. Serve hot.

SCALLOPED CARROTS AND CELERY

1 teaspoon vegetable oil	1 small onion, peeled and thinly sliced
1 large or two small carrots, trimmed, scraped, washed, and thinly sliced	1 tablespoon flour
	Salt and freshly ground black pepper
1 stalk celery, trimmed, washed, and thinly sliced	3 tablespoons milk

1. Pour the oil into a small heavy pot with a cover.
2. Layer the vegetables in the pot one at a time. Sprinkle each layer with flour and salt and pepper to taste.
3. Pour the milk over all, cover, cook over very low heat until the vegetables are fork-tender.

CARROT AND CORN PUDDING

½ ear of corn cut from the cob
2 small carrots, trimmed, scraped, washed and diced
1 egg

1 tablespoon cream
Salt and freshly ground black pepper
Butter

1. In a small bowl mix the corn kernels, diced carrots, egg and cream. Add salt and pepper to taste and mix again.
2. Preheat oven to 350 degrees.
3. Grease a small baking dish with butter. Pour the vegetable mixture into the prepared dish.
4. Bake for 1 hour.

CREAMED CARROTS AND CELERY

1 or 2 carrots
1 stalk celery
Water
Salt and freshly ground black pepper

1 tablespoon butter
⅛ teaspoon nutmeg
¼ teaspoon sugar
¼ cup light cream

1. Trim and wash the carrots and celery and cut them into small cubes. There should be about ¼ cup celery and ½ cup carrots.
2. Place the vegetables in a small heavy pot with a cover. Add salted water just to cover and bring to a boil. Cover and cook for about 10 minutes. Do not overcook.
3. Drain the cooked carrots and celery through a sieve. Put the butter into the empty pot and let it melt. Stir in the drained celery and carrots and season with salt, nutmeg, and sugar. Pour in the cream and mix well. Simmer for about 5 minutes, stirring and shaking frequently. Serve hot.

CREAMED CARROTS AND TURNIPS

2 medium-sized carrots, trimmed, scraped, washed, and diced	Salt and freshly ground black pepper
2 small-sized turnips, pared, washed, and diced	½ teaspoon sugar
Water	2 teaspoons butter
	1 tablespoon light cream
	Paprika

1. Put the diced carrots, and turnips in a saucepan with a cover and barely cover with water. Season to taste with salt, pepper, and sugar. Cover the vegetables and cook for 15 minutes, or until tender.
2. Pour off any remaining water if any and stir in the butter and cream. Let heat through. Sprinkle with paprika and serve hot.

CARROTS IN LEMON JUICE

1 or 2 carrots, trimmed, scraped, washed, and sliced	Salt and freshly ground black pepper
2 teaspoons butter	2 teaspoons chopped shallots
	1 tablespoon lemon juice

1. In a small heavy pot sauté the carrots in butter over medium heat for 10 to 15 minutes, or until a little browned, and almost done, but not overcooked. Stir frequently.
2. Add the shallots and lemon juice. Blend and cook for another minute. Add salt and pepper to taste. Serve hot with the natural lemon glaze.

BRAISED CARROTS

2 medium-sized carrots, trimmed, scraped, washed, and thinly sliced	Salt and freshly ground black pepper to taste 2 teaspoons butter

1. Heat the butter in a small heavy pot with cover. Add the carrots and sprinkle them with salt and pepper to taste.
2. Cover the pot and put it on a Flame-Tamer over very low heat.
3. Cook for about ½ hour, or until the carrots are fork-tender.

GLAZED CARROTS

3 medium-small carrots, trimmed, scraped, washed, and thinly sliced Water	2 teaspoons butter ½ teaspoon sugar Salt and freshly ground black pepper

1. Put the carrots in a small heavy pot with a cover. Add water just to cover. Add the sugar, butter and salt and pepper to taste.
2. Cover the pot and cook over low heat for about 10 minutes. Uncover and turn up the heat. Cook until all the water has evaporated. Stir gently and let the carrots glaze well. Serve hot.

PUREE OF CELERY ROOT

1 small celery root, pared and washed	1 very small onion, peeled
	Water
1 tablespoon butter	2 tablespoons light cream
Salt and freshly ground black pepper	

1. Dice or thinly slice the celery root and onion so they will cook quickly.
2. Put the vegetables in a saucepan with a cover and add water to cover. Bring the water to a boil, partially cover the saucepan, and cook over medium heat for about 20 minutes, or until tender.
3. Drain the vegetables and purée in a food processor, blender, or food mill.
4. Season the purée with salt and pepper to taste, butter, and cream. Combine well and serve hot.

CAULIFLOWER WITH PIMIENTO-CHEESE SAUCE

1 teaspoon butter	1 tablespoon chopped pimiento
1 teaspoon flour	Salt and freshly ground black
¼ cup milk	pepper
2 tablespoons grated Cheddar cheese	1 very small cauliflower

1. Melt the butter in a small saucepan and stir in the flour. Cook for a minute and stir in the milk. Continue to stir until the sauce thickens. Stir in the cheese and the pimiento. Mix well and blend in the cheese as it melts. Season with salt and pepper to taste. Set aside and keep warm.
2. Simmer the cauliflower in salted water until just tender. Drain and serve hot with the sauce.

SCALLOPED CAULIFLOWER

2 teaspoons butter
6 cauliflower flowerettes
6 crackers
Salt and freshly ground black pepper to taste

¼ cup grated Parmesan cheese or shredded Cheddar or Gruyere cheese
⅓ cup light cream

1. Butter the bottom and sides of a small baking dish with ½ teaspoon of the butter.
2. Slice the cauliflower thinly so that it will lie flat in the baking dish.
3. Crumble 2 crackers and spread them over the bottom of the baking dish. Cover with slices of cauliflower and season with salt and pepper to taste.
4. Repeat step 3 twice more.
5. Top the layers with cheese and pour cream over all. Dot with the remaining butter.
6. Preheat the oven to 300 degrees.
7. Bake for 40 minutes, or until the cauliflower is tender but not overcooked. Uncover for the last 10 minutes, or put under the broiler to brown the top of the scallop, if desired.

SUCCOTASH

1 tablespoon dry navy beans
1 slice of bacon
1 small onion, peeled and chopped
1 small green pepper, cored and chopped
1 small potato, peeled and chopped
Water

1 small tomato, cored, peeled and chopped
1 teaspoon sugar
Salt and freshly ground black pepper
1 ear of fresh corn, shucked and the kernels cut off the cob
Butter

1. Put the beans in a saucepan with a cover. Add water to cover the beans and soak them for 4 hours, or overnight. Boil the beans gently until they are tender. Set aside.
2. Fry the bacon until completely rendered of its fat. Remove the bacon and reserve it.
3. Pour off all but 1 tablespoon of bacon fat in the skillet and sauté the chopped onion and green pepper until the onion is translucent. Add the potato and cook for another minute.
4. Combine the beans with the tomato and onion, green pepper, and potato mixture. Season with sugar, and salt and pepper to taste.
5. Add the kernels of corn and simmer for 1 minute. Serve hot, adding butter, if desired.

CURRIED CORN

1 ear of fresh corn	1 teaspoon vinegar
1 tablespoon butter	½ teaspoon sugar
1 tablespoon chopped onions	Salt and freshly ground black
1 teaspoon curry powder	pepper

1. Shuck the ear of corn and clean it of all silks. Cut off the ends of the cob.
2. With a sharp paring knife cut the kernels from the cob and discard the cob.
3. Melt the butter in a small skillet, with a cover. Stir in the chopped onion. Cook for 1 minute, stirring, and add the curry powder, vinegar, sugar, and salt and pepper to taste. Mix well and cook for 1 more minute.
4. Add the corn, cover the skillet, and cook over very low heat for two minutes. Serve hot.

CORN PUDDING—1

1 ear of corn	2 tablespoons milk
2 teaspoons butter, melted	Salt and freshly ground black
1 egg yolk	pepper

1. Shuck the ear of corn, remove the silks, and trim the ends of the ear. With a sharp paring knife cut down the center of each kernel turning the cob to complete the incisions.
2. Turn the knife to the dull side and scrape down the cob to release the corn milk. Scrape well but do not incorporate husk or skin. Discard the cob and clinging emptied kernels.
3. Coat the bottom and sides of a small baking dish with the melted butter.
4. In a small bowl, mix the corn milk, egg yolk, and milk with salt and pepper to taste.
5. Preheat the oven to 350 degrees.
6. Pour the mixture into the prepared dish and bake for 40 minutes.

CORN PUDDING—2

Butter	Salt and freshly ground black
½ ear of corn cut off the cob	pepper
1 egg	2 teaspoons onion, minced

1. Butter a small baking dish, and set it aside.
2. In a small bowl, mix the corn, onion, and egg with salt and pepper to taste. Pour the mixture into the prepared baking dish.
3. Preheat the oven to 350 degrees.
4. Bake for 1 hour.

BRAISED CORN

1 ear of corn
1 teaspoon butter
1 small white onion, peeled, sliced, and separated into rings

Salt and freshly ground black pepper

1. Cut the corn kernels off the cob.
2. Butter a small heavy pot with a cover.
3. Add the corn, onion, and salt and pepper to taste to the pot. Cover tightly and stirring occasionally, cook, over very low heat for 20 minutes, or until the onion is nearly tender. Serve hot.

CORN, ZUCCHINI, AND CHEESE CASSEROLE

1 ear of fresh corn
1 teaspoon butter
2 tablespoons chopped onion
½ clove of garlic, peeled and minced
1 small zucchini, trimmed, washed, and cut into thin slices
1 egg

2 tablespoons milk
¼ cup cream
Salt and freshly ground black pepper to taste
1 shake nutmeg
1 tablespoon grated Cheddar cheese
Butter

1. Preheat the oven to 375 degrees.
2. Cut the corn kernels off the cob and set aside.
3. Melt the butter in a small skillet and sauté the garlic and onion. Add the zucchini and cook for a minute or so.
4. In a small bowl blend the egg, milk, and cream and nutmeg and salt and pepper to taste. Add the corn and cheese. Mix well. Combine with the seasoned zucchini and mix well.
5. Grease a baking dish with the butter and pour in the pudding mixture. Bake for 30 minutes and serve hot.

VIRGINIA CREAMED CORN

Inspired by a casserole served by Virginia Shoop Knox.

Butter to grease the casserole
1   8½-ounce can cream-style corn
1   medium-sized pepper prefer-
    ably the slim Italian type

Salt and freshly ground black
pepper

1. Grease a small baking dish with the butter.
2. Empty the can of cream style corn into the prepared dish.
3. Slice the pepper into ¼-inch rings. Remove the seeds and any internal white ribs. Discard the ends of the pepper.
4. Put the pepper rings on top of the corn and season the casserole with salt and pepper to taste.
5. Preheat the oven to 350 degrees.
6. Bake for 30 minutes. Serve hot.

FRESH CORN LOAF

Butter
1   ear of fresh corn
1   small tomato, peeled, cored,
    and chopped
1   small onion, peeled and
    chopped
1   small green pepper, cored,
    seeded, and chopped

¼   cup yellow cornmeal
¼   cup grated Cheddar cheese
1   egg
¼   cup milk
    Salt and freshly ground black
    pepper
    Paprika

1. Butter a small baking dish.
2. Cut the kernels from the corncob and put them in a mixing bowl. Add the tomato, onion, green pepper, cornmeal, cheese, egg, milk, and salt, pepper, and paprika to taste. Mix well and pour the mixture into the prepared baking dish.
3. Preheat the oven to 375 degrees.
4. Bake for 1 hour and serve hot with additional butter, if desired.

GREEN BEAN AND
POTATO PUREE AU GRATIN

¼ pound green beans, washed and
trimmed of ends and strings
and cut in 1-inch lengths

1 medium-sized or 2 small-sized
potatoes
Salt

2 teaspoons butter plus butter
for the baking dish
Pinch of nutmeg

2 tablespoons grated Parmesan
or Swiss cheese

1. Preheat the oven to 450 degrees.
2. Put the green beans in a saucepan with a cover. Add water to cover the beans. Add a little salt and bring to a boil.
3. Meanwhile peel the potatoes and cut them into 1-inch cubes. When the beans begin to boil, add the potatoes. Cover the saucepan and cook over low heat for about 15 minutes. Do not overcook. Drain well.
4. Purée the drained bean and potato mixture to a fine texture in a food processor, blender, or food mill.
5. Add butter, nutmeg, and salt to taste. Blend once more.
6. Butter a small baking dish.
7. Pour the purée into the prepared dish and top with the cheese. Bake for 20 minutes and serve hot.

COUNTRY VEGETABLES

⅔ cup trimmed green beans in
1-inch lengths

2 small white onions, peeled

2 small new potatoes, peeled

1 teaspoon bacon drippings or
1 slice of bacon, diced
Salt and freshly ground black
pepper to taste
Water to cover

1. Put all ingredients in a small heavy pot with a cover. Cover the pot and simmer over low heat for about 20 minutes, or until the vegetables are fork-tender. Let stand until serving time.
2. Before serving, heat to hot and taste for seasonings. Adjust to taste with additional salt and pepper, if necessary.

JUST-COOKED GREEN BEANS

½ cup water
2 teaspoons vinegar
1 small onion, cut in thin slices
   separated into rings
¾ pound green beans, trimmed of
   ends and any strings

Salt to taste
1 tablespoon bacon drippings or
   1 slice of bacon cut into ½-inch
   dice

1. In a saucepan with a cover, mix the water, vinegar, and onion rings. Put the pan over medium heat and bring to a boil.
2. Reduce the heat and add the beans. Simmer, covered, for about 10 minutes, until tender but not overcooked. Uncover.
3. Season with salt and add the bacon drippings or bacon. Bring to a boil again and cook over medium-high heat for 4 or 5 minutes. The beans should be undercooked or al dente.

ITALIAN GREEN BEANS

¼ pound green beans
1 clove garlic, peeled and
   crushed
2 tablespoons red wine vinegar

2 teaspoons olive oil
   Salt and freshly ground black
   pepper

1. Trim the ends off the beans and remove any strings. Cut the beans into 1-inch lengths.
2. Put the beans in a saucepan and cover them with water. Add a little salt. Bring to a boil, reduce the heat, and simmer for 20 minutes. Drain the beans.
3. Combine the garlic, vinegar, and olive oil with salt and pepper to taste. Mix the sauce and pour it over the beans and let stand for at least 1 hour.
4. At serving time heat the beans gently and serve warm.

STUFFED GREEN PEPPER MAGYAR

1 large green pepper
3 ounces ground chuck or round
1 small onion, peeled and finely chopped
1 tablespoon rice
Salt and freshly ground black pepper to taste
1 teaspoon butter

1 teaspoon flour
4 tablespoons tomato sauce
4 tablespoons water
¼ teaspoon paprika
¼ teaspoon sugar
2 tablespoons cooked peas (optional)

1. Remove the top of the green pepper and scoop out the seeds and white ribs, leaving a large space for stuffing. Wash well.
2. In a small bowl mix together the ground meat, rice, onion, and salt and pepper.
3. Stuff the pepper loosely, but not to the top. Leave some space. Put in small heavy pot with a cover, which you have lined with aluminum foil and if necessary crushed in such a way as to make a nest to hold the pepper upright.
4. Heat the butter in a small pan and add the flour. Stir over low heat for 1 minute. Then add the tomato sauce, water, paprika, and sugar. Mix well and taste for seasonings, adding more salt or pepper as needed.
5. Pour the sauce around pepper in the casserole and cook, covered, over low heat for 1 hour, or until the pepper is fork-tender.
6. Add the cooked peas, if desired and heat through.

Note: If there is extra stuffing after filling the pepper, make a small round ball or two of the extra and add to the casserole.

DUXELLES

The favorite use for duxelles is in stuffing for meat or fowl, but I like them warm as a vegetable.

1 tablespoon butter	Salt and freshly ground black
2 tablespoons finely chopped	pepper
onion	Pinch of nutmeg
⅔ cup finely chopped mushrooms	

1. Melt the butter in a small skillet and add the onions. Stir over low heat and cook until golden but not brown.
2. Add the chopped mushrooms to the onions. Stir frequently and cook over the same low heat until the mushroom liquid is almost completely evaporated.
3. Season to taste with salt and freshly ground black pepper and a pinch of nutmeg. Blend well and cool.

BAKED MUSHROOMS

This is good for leftover mushrooms.

6 or 7 mushrooms	Salt and paprika
2 teaspoons butter	2 tablespoons cream

1. Remove the stems from the mushrooms, and discard them. Wash the caps in cold water.
2. Place a sheet of aluminum foil in a small baking dish and oil the foil well.
3. Put the mushrooms on the oiled foil cap side up and dot with butter. Add salt and paprika to taste.
4. Preheat the oven to 400 degrees.
5. Pour the cream around the mushrooms and bake for 10 minutes.

MUSHROOMS AU GRATIN

5 medium-sized fresh mushrooms	¼ cup milk
2 teaspoons butter	Paprika garnish
Salt	1 tablespoon Parmesan cheese
1 teaspoon flour	or bread crumbs

1. Remove the stems from the mushrooms and discard them. Peel the mushroom caps and wash them in cold water. Put the mushrooms in a paper towel and dry them well. Cut them in quarters.
2. Melt the butter in a small skillet and when it is hot add the mushrooms with salt to taste. Stir or shake the skillet and cook the mushrooms over medium heat for 2 minutes.
3. Sprinkle the mushrooms with flour and stir to coat them well.
4. Pour in the milk and stir until the sauce begins to thicken.
5. Lightly grease a small baking dish.
6. Put the mushrooms and sauce in the prepared dish. Sprinkle the top with Parmesan cheese and put under the broiler for a minute, or until browned.

OKRA AND TOMATO STEW

1 tablespoon butter	Salt to taste
1 tablespoon chopped onion	¼ teaspoon paprika
1 cup okra, trimmed, washed, and sliced	Pinch of curry powder
1 medium-sized fresh tomato, cored, peeled, and chopped	½ teaspoon brown sugar

1. Melt the butter in a skillet and add the onion. Sauté until the onion is wilted.
2. Add the okra and sauté, stirring, for another 4 or 5 minutes.
3. Add the tomato and seasonings. Bring to a boil and simmer until the okra is tender. Taste and adjust the seasonings, if necessary.

PUREED PEAS IN ONION SHELL

1 large onion, peeled
½ cup cooked fresh or canned peas
1 tablespoon butter

Salt and freshly ground black pepper
1 teaspoon sugar
Butter

1. Boil the onion in water to cover for about 50 minutes, or until it is just tender. Do not overcook.
2. Slice a thin slice from the top of the cooked onion. Insert a knife in the onion about ½ inch from the outside, and cut out a cavity for the stuffing. Remove and discard the onion pulp.
3. Purée the peas in a food processor, blender, or food mill. Season to taste with butter, salt and pepper, and sugar. Spoon the purée into the hollowed-out onion. Top with a pat of butter.
4. Heat in the broiler until the onion and purée are hot.

SCALLOPED ONION AND CELERY

6 saltine crackers, in crumbs
1 stalk celery, trimmed, washed, and diced
1 small white onion, peeled, thinly sliced, and separated into rings

Salt and freshly ground black pepper
2 teaspoons butter plus butter for the pot
1 tablespoon cream

1. Butter a small heavy pot with a cover. Sprinkle half the cracker crumbs on the bottom of the pot.
2. Add the diced celery and then the onion rings.
3. Top with the remaining cracker crumbs. Dot with butter and sprinkle with salt and pepper to taste.
4. Pour the cream over all and cover. Put on a Flame-Tamer and cook over very low heat for about 25 minutes, or until the vegetables are tender.

BRAISED PARSNIP

2 teaspoons butter	Salt and freshly ground black
1 small parsnip, pared and thinly sliced	pepper
	Brown sugar

1. Put the butter and thinly sliced parsnip in a small heavy pot with a cover. Sprinkle with salt, pepper, and brown sugar to taste.
2. Cook, covered, over the lowest possible heat for ½ hour, or until tender. Shake the casserole shortly after starting to braise. Serve hot or warm.

PARSNIP PUREE

This is good for a change of pace.

1 medium-sized parsnip, pared and cut into julienne strips	Salt and freshly ground black pepper to taste
Water	2 teaspoons butter
	¼ teaspoon nutmeg

1. Put the parsnip in a saucepan. Add water just to cover and salt and pepper to taste. Simmer until tender. Drain the parsnip and purée in a food mill, food processor, or blender.
2. At serving time add the butter and nutmeg. Blend well and taste for seasoning. Add more salt and pepper, if desired.

PEAS AND CARROT PUREE

1   carrot, trimmed, scraped,
    washed, and cut into very thin
    slices
⅔ cup shelled fresh peas

Water
2   teaspoons butter
    Salt and freshly ground black
    pepper to taste

1. Put the carrot and peas in a saucepan and just barely cover them with water. Bring to a boil and simmer for about 20 minutes, or until tender.
2. Drain the vegetables and purée them in a food mill, blender, or food processor. Season with butter and salt and pepper to taste. Serve hot.

STEWED PEAS

⅔ cup shelled fresh peas
1   tablespoon chopped pimiento
1   small onion, peeled, sliced,
    and separated into rings
1   stalk celery with leaves,
    trimmed, washed, and finely
    chopped

1   teaspoon sugar
1   teaspoon butter
    Salt and freshly ground black
    pepper

Put the peas, pimiento, onion rings, celery, sugar, butter and salt and pepper to taste into a saucepan with a cover. Cook, covered, over the lowest heat possible until the peas are tender.

POTATO-CARROT PUREE

1 medium-sized potato, peeled, washed, and quartered	1 small onion, peeled and sliced
1 medium-sized carrot, trimmed, scraped, washed, and sliced	1 tablespoon butter or to taste
	½ cup milk or cream
	Salt to taste

1. Put the potato, carrot, and onion in a saucepan and cover with water. Add a little salt and bring to a boil. Simmer for 20 minutes, or until the vegetables are tender.
2. Drain and purée the vegetables in a food mill, food processor, or blender.
3. Season with butter, milk, and salt to taste. Serve hot.

POTATOES LYONNAISE

1 or 2 new potatoes	1 teaspoon vegetable oil
Salt and freshly ground black pepper	2 tablespoons chopped onion
2 teaspoons butter	Chopped parsley

1. Wash the potatoes well, scraping off any blemishes. Drop the potatoes in boiling water to cover. Add salt to taste and cook for 15 minutes, or until almost tender, but not completely cooked. Drain and let cool.
2. When the potatoes are cool, peel and slice them thinly, but with enough thickness to hold together in further cooking.
3. Put 1 teaspoon butter and 1 teaspoon oil in a skillet and, when hot, sauté the potatoes to a light brown, shaking the pan and turning the potatoes once.
4. In another skillet, sauté the chopped onion in the remaining butter for about 2 minutes. They should be rather crunchy, so do not overcook.
5. Combine the potatoes and the onions. Mix together without breaking up the potatoes. Serve with a sprinkling of parsley.

STUFFED POTATO

1 large baking potato	Salt and freshly ground black
2 teaspoons butter	pepper
1 small onion, peeled and finely	1 egg
chopped	2 tablespoons tomato sauce
¼ pound ground beef	½ cup beef broth

1. Bake the potato in a 350 degree oven for 1 hour, or until tender.
2. In a small skillet, melt 1 teaspoon butter and sauté the onion until it is translucent. Add the meat and salt and pepper to taste, and cook for 10 minutes, stirring occasionally to prevent sticking. Set aside.
3. Cut the potato in half lengthwise and carefully scoop out the flesh, leaving a cavity for the stuffing.
4. Mash the potato flesh and mix it with the egg, salt and pepper to taste, and the remaining butter. Mix in the meat mixture and stir until smooth. Stuff the prepared potato shells, heaping the stuffing high, if necessary. Put the stuffed potato in a small casserole.
5. Preheat the oven to 350 degrees.
6. Simmer the tomato sauce and beef broth together in a small saucepan. Check for seasonings, and add salt and pepper, if necessary. Pour the sauce around the stuffed potatoes in the casserole.
7. Bake, uncovered, for 25 minutes.

VENETIAN-STYLE POTATOES

1 tablespoon butter	2 tablespoons chopped parsley
2 tablespoons chopped onion	Salt and freshly ground black
1 cup diced, peeled potatoes	pepper

1. Melt the butter in a skillet. Add the onion and cook, stirring constantly, until the onion is translucent, about 1 minute.
2. Add the potatoes, stir and mix well, and cook, stirring occasionally, for about 20 minutes, or until the potatoes are fork-tender.
3. Add the parsley and salt and pepper to taste and mix well. Serve immediately.

SCALLOPED SALSIFY

1 medium-sized salsify, pared and thinly sliced	4 saltine crackers, crumbled Salt and freshly ground black
Lemon juice	pepper
2 teaspoons butter	1 tablespoon cream

1. Slice the pared salsify into a bowl of cold water and add a few drops of lemon juice. Let set until you are ready to prepare the dish.
2. Use a small heavy pot with a cover to melt 1 teaspoon of butter. Sprinkle half the cracker crumbs on the bottom of the pan. Top with slices of salsify. Sprinkle the remaining cracker crumbs over the salsify.
3. Dot the remaining butter over the cracker crumbs and sprinkle salt and pepper to taste over all. Pour the cream over all.
4. Cover and cook over very low heat for ½ hour, or until tender. You may want to use a Flame-Tamer for this. If you prefer, you can bake the salsify in a covered baking dish at 350 degrees for ½ hour. Add more cream if the dish becomes too dry.

BAKED SPINACH

2 teaspoons olive oil	½ pound fresh spinach, picked
1 clove of garlic, peeled and	over, washed, and drained
minced	Salt and freshly ground black
	pepper

1. Preheat the oven to 375 degrees.
2. Oil the bottom of a casserole with a cover. Add the garlic, spinach, and salt and pepper to taste.
3. Cover and bake for 25 minutes. Serve as is or with vinegar.

SPINACH WITH PARMESAN CHEESE

½ a 10-ounce package of fresh	½ clove garlic, peeled and minced
spinach, trimmed of tough	Salt and crushed red pepper
stems and well washed	flakes to taste
Water	1 tablespoon grated Parmesan
2 teaspoons butter	cheese
2 teaspoons olive oil	

1 Shred the spinach coarsely.
2. In a saucepan, bring water to cover and salt to taste to a boil and add the spinach. When the water returns to a boil, cook for 30 seconds and drain the spinach well in a colander. Press out water that doesn't drain out. Place the drained spinach in a baking dish.
3. Melt the butter and oil in a small skillet and stir in the minced garlic and add salt and crushed red pepper flakes to taste. Stir and cook for about 4 minutes.
4. Pour the oil mixture over the spinach in the casserole and sprinkle the top with Parmesan cheese. Put in a preheated broiler for about 10 minutes, or until brown on top.

VINEGAR-BAKED SPINACH

½ bag packed spinach
2 strips bacon, diced
1 small onion, peeled and
chopped

2 tablespoons red wine vinegar
Salt and freshly ground black
pepper
½ teaspoon sugar

1. Wash the spinach well in lots of cold water. Discard any tough stems. Drain the spinach well and put it in a casserole with a cover. Set aside.
2. Preheat the oven to 350 degrees.
3. In a skillet, fry the bacon until it is well cooked, but not crisp. Pour off and discard most of the drippings.
4. Add the chopped onion to the skillet and sauté for 1 minute with bacon.
5. Add the wine vinegar to the skillet and season the mixture with salt and pepper to taste. Add the sugar and mix well. Bring to a boil and pour over the spinach.
6. Bake for 30 minutes, or until the spinach is tender.

SCALLOPED SQUASH

2 teaspoons butter
1 small onion, peeled and thinly
sliced
1 small yellow squash, trimmed,
washed, and thinly sliced

5 saltine crackers, crumbled
Salt and freshly ground black
pepper
¼ cup cream
Paprika

1. Preheat the oven to 350 degrees.
2. Butter a small baking dish with a little of the butter. Layer half the onions, then the squash, and then the crumbled cracker crumbs in the baking dish. Sprinkle with salt and pepper to taste. Repeat the layers. Season the top layer with more salt and pepper. Dot the top of the casserole with the remaining butter and pour the cream over all. Sprinkle with paprika.
3. Bake for 30 minutes. Serve hot.

YELLOW SQUASH SAUCE ANN

1 small yellow squash, peeled,
   washed, and sliced
2 tablespoons tomato purée
1 small onion, peeled and sliced

1 teaspoon soy sauce
   Salt and freshly ground black
   pepper
2 teaspoons cream

1. Put the squash in a small heavy pot with a cover.
2. Add the tomato purée and top with the slices of onion. Season with soy sauce and salt and pepper to taste.
3. Cook, covered, over very low heat until the vegetables are almost tender, but not mushy.
4. Add the cream. Mix well and serve hot.

CHEESE SOUFFLE IN TOMATO SHELLS

2 medium-sized tomatoes,
   washed
1 teaspoon butter
1 teaspoon flour
½ cup milk
2 dashes Worcestershire sauce

¼ cup grated Cheddar or Gruyere
   cheese
   Salt and freshly ground black
   pepper
1 egg, separated

1. Cut the tops off the tomatoes and scoop out the inside pulp to form a case for stuffing. Discard the tomato pulp or save it to use in another dish.
2. Melt the butter in a small saucepan and stir in the flour. Add the milk and stir until the mixture begins to thicken. Season with Worcestershire sauce and salt and pepper to taste. Add the cheese and stir until the cheese melts.
3. Add a little cheese sauce to the egg yolk and mix well. Then combine this mixture with the rest of the cheese sauce and mix well.
4. Beat the egg white until it is stiff. Carefully fold the egg white into the cheese sauce.

5. Preheat the oven to 400 degrees.
6. Fill the prepared tomato cases with the soufflé mixture. Bake for 20 minutes. Serve immediately.

BROILED TOMATO HALVES

1 very ripe medium-sized tomato
2 pinches dried basil or 1 teaspoon chopped basil

Salt and freshly ground black pepper
1 teaspoon butter

1. Wash and dry the tomato and cut it in half. Put the halves in a small ovenproof pan.
2. Season the tomato halves with basil and salt and pepper to taste.
3. Add half the butter to each half and broil at 400 degrees for 5 minutes. Serve hot.

Note: For a taste change, you can substitute dried oregano for the basil.

SCALLOPED TOMATO—1

1 medium-sized tomato
1 slice trimmed white bread, crumbled

Salt and freshly ground black pepper
2 teaspoons butter

1. Put the tomato in a small saucepan and cover with water. Bring to a boil. Let the tomato rest in the hot water for ½ minute. Remove it, then peel, core, and dice it.
2. Butter a small baking dish and add one half the diced tomato. Cover the tomato with one half the bread crumbs. Repeat with the remaining tomato and crumbs. Sprinkle with salt and pepper to taste. Dot with butter and broil until the top crumbs are golden. Serve hot.

SCALLOPED TOMATO—2

2 teaspoons butter
6 saltine crackers
1 small or medium-sized tomato

Salt and freshly ground black
pepper to taste
1 tablespoon light cream
¼ teaspoon dried basil

1. Grease a small casserole with a bit of the butter.
2. Crumble 3 of the crackers, and sprinkle them over the bottom of the greased casserole.
3. Bring the tomato to a boil in water to cover. Remove the tomato and peel, core, and slice it thinly.
4. Preheat the oven to 350 degrees.
5. Cover the crumbs in the casserole with half the tomato slices. Season with salt and pepper to taste.
6. Repeat the layers with the remaining crumbled crackers and the remaining tomato slices. Season with salt and pepper to taste.
7. Dot the top layer with the remaining butter and pour the cream over all. Sprinkle the top with the basil.
8. Bake for 30 minutes.

MOLDED YELLOW TURNIPS

1 small yellow turnip, scraped
and cut into 1-inch cubes
Water
Salt and freshly ground black
pepper

Pinch of nutmeg
1 tablespoon cream
1 egg yolk
Butter

1. Put the turnip in a saucepan and cover it with water. Add salt to taste. Bring to a boil and simmer for about 15 minutes, or until the turnip is tender but not mushy.
2. Preheat the oven to 375 degrees.
3. Drain the turnip and pass it through a food processor or food mill very casually so as to leave some body to the vegetable. Do not purée.

4. Now place the turnip in a mixing bowl and add the nutmeg and pepper. Mix well but carefully.
5. Blend the cream and the egg yolk and add them to the mixing bowl. Stir again carefully and test the seasoning. Add more salt, if desired.
6. Butter a small baking dish. Pour in the turnip and cream mixture. Set the baking dish in a larger pan and pour in ¼ inch hot water.
7. Bake for about 45 minutes. Unmold the pudding and serve hot.

CHEESE-STUFFED TURNIP

1 medium-sized turnip	1 tablespoon chopped tomato
Salt and freshly ground black pepper to taste	1 tablespoon shredded Swiss cheese
Lemon juice	½ teaspoon sugar
1 tablespoon butter	Finely chopped parsley
1 tablespoon chopped onion	

1. Peel the turnip and remove the center to prepare a shell with a side wall of about ½ inch. A melon ball cutter is recommended for this.
2. Boil the turnip shell in salted water with lemon juice added for 30 minutes. Drain and cool.
3. Melt the butter in a skillet and add the chopped onion and a tablespoon or so of the reserved scooped out center of the turnip, which you have chopped rather finely. Stir and cook until tender.
4. Add salt, tomato, shredded cheese, sugar, and pepper and blend.
5. Salt the turnip shell inside and fill the cavity with the cheese and vegetable mixture. Sprinkle the top with a little more shredded cheese.
6. Place the stuffed turnip in a small casserole with a cover. Support it with crinkled aluminum foil if necessary to prevent its falling on a side. Let it stand upright. Bake the stuffed turnip for 20 minutes and garnish with parsley.

PUREE OF CARROT AND TURNIP
IN TURNIP SHELL

1 medium-sized turnip, peeled	2 teaspoons butter
1 small carrot, scraped, washed, and diced	½ teaspoon sugar
Salt and freshly ground black pepper to taste	1 tablespoon grated Parmesan cheese

1. Cook the turnip for ½ hour in salted boiling water. Let it cool.
2. Hollow out the turnip, leaving a shell about ½ inch thick. Salt the shell inside. Retain the scooped out center of the turnip.
3. Cook the peeled and diced carrot until tender and purée the carrot and the turnip center. Blend the purée and season it with salt and pepper, sugar and butter. Stuff the cavity in the turnip with the purée and top with cheese.
4. Preheat the oven to 375 degrees.
5. Place the stuffed turnip in a small casserole. Nest it in crumbled aluminum foil, if necessary, to hold it upright. Bake for ½ hour.

BRAISED TURNIP

1 small turnip, peeled and thinly sliced	Salt to taste
1 small onion, peeled and thinly sliced	Paprika
	2 teaspoons butter

1. Layer the vegetables in a small heavy casserole with a cover. Sprinkle them with salt and paprika to taste. Dot them with the butter.
2. Cover and put on a Flame-Tamer. Simmer over very low heat until tender. You can also bake in the oven for 30 minutes at 400 degrees.

SCALLOPED ZUCCHINI

2 teaspoons cooking oil
6 saltine crackers, crumbled
1 small zucchini, trimmed, washed, and thinly sliced
1 small onion, peeled and thinly sliced

Salt and freshly ground black pepper
2 teaspoons butter
2 tablespoons cream

1. Oil the bottom and sides of a small heavy pot with a cover.
2. Put half the crumbled crackers in the bottom of the oiled pot. Layer the sliced zucchini and onion on the cracker crumbs. Season with salt and pepper to taste. Top with the remaining crumbs.
3. Dot the top of the casserole with bits of butter and pour the cream over all. Cover tightly and put over a Flame-Tamer. Cook for 20 minutes, or until the zucchini is tender. Serve hot.

STEWED ZUCCHINI

2 teaspoons butter
1 medium-sized carrot, trimmed, scraped, washed, and thinly sliced

1 small zucchini, trimmed, washed, and thinly sliced
Salt and freshly ground black pepper
1 teaspoon finely chopped parsley

1. Heat the butter in a heavy skillet with a cover and add the carrot slices with salt and pepper to taste. Cover and cook over low heat for about 4 or 5 minutes.
2. Add the zucchini and cover again. Cook for another 4 or 5 minutes or until both vegetables are almost done. They should preferably be undercooked a bit.
3. Shake the pan well and add the parsley and salt and pepper, if necessary. Serve hot.

BRAISED ZUCCHINI—1

1 tablespoon butter
1 small zucchini, pared, washed, and sliced
1 small Italian-style green pepper, cored, seeded, and sliced

5 cherry tomatoes, halved, or an equal quantity of chopped fresh tomato
Salt and freshly ground black pepper

1. Melt the butter in a small heavy pot with a tight-fitting cover.
2. Add the zucchini, pepper, tomatoes, and salt and pepper to taste.
3. Cover the casserole tightly and put it over the lowest possible heat. Cook until the vegetables are fork-tender. Serve hot.

BRAISED ZUCCHINI—2

1 small zucchini, trimmed of ends and sliced in half
Salt and freshly ground black pepper

3 tablespoons grated Cheddar cheese

1. Put the zucchini halves in a small heavy pot just large enough to fit them snugly.
2. Season the zucchini with salt and pepper to taste and sprinkle the cheese over the cut tops.
3. Cover the pot and put over the lowest possible heat. Cook until fork-tender. Serve hot.

Salads

A crisp, freshly-prepared salad is a delight, whether served as a main course or as an accompaniment to another dish. A simple tossed, green salad topped with Mayonnaise, Bacon, and Green Onion Dressing is easily adapted to a single serving, as are many of the other salads suggested here. Try a Beef Salad Vinaigrette, a Shrimp and Potato Salad, or a Waldorf-style Salad, for variety.

BEEF SALAD VINAIGRETTE

½ cup cooked beef, cut into ¼-inch cubes
1 small center rib of celery, trimmed, washed, and cut into small dice
1 tablespoon chopped onion
½ cup peeled and chopped tomato
2 cornichons, sliced thinly or about 2 tablespoons sour pickles

¼ clove garlic, peeled and finely minced
1 teaspoon chopped parsley
Chopped greens
1 teaspoon imported French or German mustard
1 teaspoon red wine vinegar
1 tablespoon vegetable oil
Salt and freshly ground black pepper

1. Put the beef, celery, onion, tomato, cornichons, garlic, and parsley into a small salad bowl and mix well.
2. Put the mustard, vinegar, and oil with salt and pepper to taste in a small jar with a close-fitting top. Shake well.
3. Pour the dressing over the salad and toss to combine. Refrigerate and serve on chopped greens.

199

EGG SALAD

1 hard-boiled egg, diced
1 tablespoon finely chopped onion
1 tablespoon mayonnaise
1 teaspoon cream

Salt
2 teaspoons chopped cornichon, or chopped olive or the same quantity of capers (optional)
Salad greens

Combine the diced egg with the onion, mayonnaise, cream, and salt to taste. Add the chopped cornichon. Mix well and refrigerate. Serve on salad greens.

LENTIL SALAD

2 tablespoons dried lentils
1 cup water
½ bay leaf
½ clove garlic, peeled
1 small white onion stuck with 1 clove
Salt and freshly ground black pepper to taste
¼ teaspoon Italian parsley
¼ teaspoon dried thyme

1 tablespoon finely chopped white onion
¼ teaspoon minced garlic
2 cherry tomatoes, diced
2 teaspoons red wine vinegar
1 teaspoon olive oil
¼ teaspoon sugar
¼ teaspoon India relish (optional)

1. Place the first 8 ingredients in a saucepan. Bring to a boil, reduce the heat, and simmer, partially covered, for 30 minutes. The lentils should retain their texture and not become mushy.
2. Drain the lentils through a sieve and discard the onion, clove, and bay leaf. Let the lentils cool.
3. To the cooled lentils add the chopped onion, minced garlic, diced tomatoes, wine vinegar, olive oil, sugar, and relish, if desired. Toss and chill before serving as a relish or as a salad on lettuce. Taste for seasonings and adjust the salt and pepper, if necessary.

SHRIMP AND POTATO SALAD

5 shrimp, cooked, peeled,
  deveined, and cut into ¼-inch
  pieces
¼ cup diced celery
1 teaspoon finely chopped dill
1 teaspoon capers
2 tablespoons mayonnaise

1 tablespoon lemon juice
1 teaspoon sugar
1 small potato, peeled, cooked,
  and diced
Salt and freshly ground pepper
  to taste
Salad greens

Mix all ingredients together and chill for ½ hour before serving on lettuce or your favorite greens.

CORN AND PIMIENTO VINAIGRETTE

1 ear of cooked corn
2 tablespoons coarsely chopped
  pimiento
1 tablespoon chopped onion
1 tablespoon chopped parsley
½ teaspoon Dijon mustard

1 teaspoon red wine vinegar
1 teaspoon lemon juice
1 tablespoon olive oil
Salt and freshly ground black
  pepper

1. Cut the kernels of corn from the cob and put them in a mixing bowl.
2. Add the pimiento, onion, and parsley.
3. In another small bowl blend the mustard, vinegar, lemon juice, and olive oil with salt and pepper to taste. Mix well and pour over the vegetables. Mix well. Refrigerate and serve cold.

BERLIN SALAD

Salad greens for one serving
3 slices of cucumber, peeled and seeded (optional)
1 small tomato, peeled and quartered (optional)

2 tablespoons canned corn kernels
2 tablespoons oil and vinegar salad dressing
Salt and freshly ground black pepper

1. Place all ingredients in a bowl and refrigerate for at least ½ hour.
2. Toss the contents of the bowl until all are coated well with dressing and serve on a chilled plate.

ALGERIAN SALAD

Salad greens in bite-sized pieces
2 tablespoons pimientos
4 anchovies
8 pitted black olives
1 teaspoon olive oil

1 teaspoon tarragon vinegar
Salt and freshly ground black pepper to taste (optional)
1 hard-cooked egg in quarters (optional)

1. Arrange the salad greens on the bottom of a cool plate. Chill until serving time.
2. At serving time, put the pimientos on the salad greens and cover them with anchovies and then black olives.
3. Season the salad with olive oil and tarragon vinegar and salt and pepper, if desired.
4. Garnish the plate with quartered hard-cooked egg, if desired.

SALAD IMPROMPTU

This is good when you have only a little leftover sour cream.

1 lettuce leaf, shredded
1 stalk celery, trimmed, washed, and cut into small cubes
½ cup diced tomato

1 teaspoon sweet pickle relish
1 tablespoon sour cream
Salt and freshly ground black pepper to taste

1. Place the shredded lettuce in a salad bowl.
2. Mix the celery, tomato, sweet pickle relish, and sour cream with salt and pepper to taste. Blend well. Taste and correct the seasonings, if necessary.
3. Spoon the mixture on the shredded lettuce and refrigerate until serving time.

DATE AND APPLE SALAD

5 dates
½ small apple, cored and diced
Lemon juice to taste

1 tablespoon mayonnaise
Lettuce

1. Pit the dates; cut them in small slices; place them in a small bowl and pour hot water over them to soften them. Let them stand ½ hour or so, or until softened.
2. Combine the dates, apple, lemon juice, and mayonnaise in a bowl. Stir and set aside in the refrigerator until serving time.
3. Serve cold on a bed of lettuce.

WILTED LETTUCE—1

2 strips bacon
2 tablespoons red wine vinegar
2 tablespoons water

2 teaspoons sugar
1 hard-cooked egg, sliced
1 cup lettuce in bite-sized pieces

1. Fry the bacon until it is crisp. Drain on a paper towel. Crumble when cool.
2. Pour off most of the drippings leaving only 1 teaspoon in the frying pan.
3. Add the vinegar, water, and sugar to the frying pan. Cook, stirring, for 1 minute.
4. Put the lettuce in a salad bowl. Top it with the egg slices and crumbled bacon. Pour the hot vinegar dressing over all. Toss and serve immediately.

WILTED LETTUCE—2

¼ pound leaf lettuce, torn into bite-sized pieces
2 or 3 strips of bacon, diced
¼ cup vinegar
1 tablespoon sugar

Salt and freshly ground black pepper
1 hard-cooked egg, sliced
3 green onions, trimmed, washed and diced

1. Place the well-washed lettuce in a small heavy pot with a cover.
2. In a skillet, fry the diced bacon until it is well rendered of its fat. Pour off all but 1 tablespoon of the bacon grease.
3. Stir the vinegar, sugar, and salt and pepper to taste into the bacon. Mix well and bring to a boil.
4. Pour the sauce over the lettuce and toss well to flavor and wilt the lettuce. Cover the casserole and place it over very low heat. A Flame-Tamer is recommended for this. This step may be omitted if you are serving the wilted lettuce immediately.
5. Top the wilted lettuce with the sliced egg and diced green onions.

COLESLAW

2 tablespoons mayonnaise
1 tablespoon vinegar
1 teaspoon sugar

¼ teaspoon celery seed (optional)
1 cup chopped cabbage

1. Thoroughly mix the mayonnaise, vinegar, sugar, and celery seed, if desired.
2. Combine the sauce with the cabbage and refrigerate before serving.

Note: Variations to this are endless. You may add pineapple, green pepper, carrot, etc., according to your taste.

WALDORF-STYLE SALAD

½ apple, diced
1 stalk celery, trimmed, washed,
   and diced
2 tablespoons whole pecans

1 tablespoon mayonnaise
1 tablespoon cream
   Shredded lettuce (optional)

1. Put the apple, celery, and pecans in a bowl.
2. Mix the mayonnaise and cream together.
3. Pour the mayonnaise mixture over the apple, celery, and pecan combination. Mix well and serve over shredded lettuce.

SOUR CREAM DRESSING

1 tablespoon sour cream
1 teaspoon vinegar
½ teaspoon sugar

¼ teaspoon dried dill weed
⅛ teaspoon salt

1. Blend all ingredients well and chill the dressing.
2. Serve over green salad or coleslaw.

MAYONNAISE, BACON, AND
GREEN ONION DRESSING

3 slices bacon
3 green onions with tops

2 tablespoons mayonnaise
2 teaspoons red wine vinegar

1. Fry the bacon until it is rendered of most of its fat. Discard the fat and cool the bacon until you can crumble it into bits.
2. Wash the green onions, carefully cutting off the root ends and peeling back the first layer of skin and discarding it. Chop them finely.
3. Combine the bacon bits, green onion, mayonnaise, and vinegar. Mix well and serve over salad greens or on crackers or toast.

Relishes and Sauces

Many dishes would be incomplete without a fresh, tangy sauce served as an accompaniment. Everyone likes to make their own taste combinations, and here are some of my favorite go-alongs.

HOT CORN RELISH

1   ear of corn
1   tablespoon vinegar
2   teaspoons sugar
2   cloves
½   teaspoon dry mustard

Dash of Worcestershire sauce
Salt and crushed red pepper
flakes to taste
2   teaspoons butter

1. Shuck the ear of corn; remove the silks and the ends of the ear. Cut off the kernels and discard the empty ear.
2. Melt the butter in a small saucepan with a cover. Add all ingredients, cover, and simmer for 10 minutes. Warm up at serving time, if necessary.

TART CRANBERRY SAUCE

1 cup raw cranberries, picked over and washed
½ cup sugar

Pinch of salt
Water

1. Put the cranberries and salt in a saucepan and cover with water. Bring to a boil and let set until cool.
2. Drain the cranberries and add the sugar and a tablespoon or so of water to dissolve the sugar. Mix well.
3. Simmer the cranberries over very low heat for ½ hour. Cool and serve with poultry, or as you desire.

CRANBERRY AND APPLE PUREE

1 cup raw cranberries, picked over and washed
1 apple, cored and sliced

½ cup water
½ cup sugar or to taste

1. Put all ingredients in a saucepan with a cover and bring to a boil. Partially cover and simmer for ½ hour. Cool.
2. Purée the mixture in a food processor or food mill.
3. Return the purée to the saucepan and add the sugar. Bring to a boil again and simmer covered for 15 minutes. Refrigerate and use as a relish or an accompaniment to hot biscuits in the morning.

PEPPER HASH

1 sweet pepper, green and turning red, cored, seeded, and washed	Boiling water
	3 tablespoons vinegar
	2 tablespoons sugar
1 medium-sized onion, peeled	Pinch of salt

1. Chop the pepper and onion coarsely.
2. Put the chopped onion and pepper in a small bowl and cover with boiling water. Let stand for 15 minutes. Drain in a bit of cheesecloth fashioned into a bag and tied with string. Hang the bag in the sink or over a catch bowl and let it drain for several hours or overnight.
3. Mix the vinegar, sugar, and salt in a small bowl or cup.
4. Put the drained pepper and onion in a small saucepan and pour the vinegar mixture over all. Bring to a boil and simmer for 10 minutes. Cool and refrigerate. Serve with sausage, ham in salad, or as you would any relish.

Note: Aunt Sallie's recipe, as I remember, calls for sweet green peppers and sweet red peppers. The above is a way of getting the attractive red and green look without preparing a large quantity of relish. In the fall one can find sweet peppers just turning green to red. The above with 1 pepper makes a half cup or so. Any left from the first serving will keep under refrigeration for a week or so.

BURGUNDY SAUCE

1 teaspoon butter	Salt and freshly ground black
1 tablespoon grated onion	pepper
2 teaspoons flour	1 teaspoon brown sugar
¼ cup Burgundy	½ teaspoon dry mustard
1 teaspoon ketchup	

1. Heat the butter in a small saucepan and sauté the onion until golden.
2. Sprinkle the onion with flour and mix well. Slowly add the Burgundy, stirring constantly.
3. Season the sauce with ketchup, salt, and pepper to taste, brown sugar, and mustard. Taste the sauce and adjust the seasonings, if necessary. Simmer the sauce for 5 minutes and keep it warm until serving time. Serve with beef.

SAUCE CHASSEUR

1 teaspoon butter	¼ teaspoon crumbled dried
2 tablespoons chopped	tarragon
mushrooms	½ teaspoon cornstarch
1 teaspoon chopped shallots	1 teaspoon water
¼ cup dry white wine	Salt and freshly ground black
1 small tomato, peeled and	pepper
chopped	

1. Melt the butter in a saucepan and add the mushrooms and shallots, and season with salt and pepper to taste. Stir and cook 4 minutes.
2. Pour in the dry white wine. Mix well and cook for 1 minute.
3. Add the tomato. Stir and cook for another minute. Taste the sauce and add sugar if the tomato is too acid.
4. Season with the tarragon. Blend the cornstarch and water and add this mixture to the sauce. Cook for about 4 minutes, stirring occasionally. Heat to hot at serving time and serve with steak, other meats, and chops.

CUCUMBER SAUCE

This goes well with salmon and other fish.

1   small or ½ medium cucumber
    Salt to taste

Paprika to taste
Vinegar to taste

1. Peel the cucumber. Cut it in half and scrape out the seeds, using a melon cutter or spoon.
2. Grate the cucumber.
3. Season to taste with salt, paprika, and vinegar.

CORNICHON AND TOMATO SAUCE

This sauce should be served over beef and other meat dishes while hot.

¼   cup chopped cornichons
2   tablespoons tomato purée
1   tablespoon water

1   teaspoon Worcestershire sauce
    Several drops of Tabasco or to
    taste

1. Put the chopped cornichons, tomato purée, water, Worcestershire sauce, and Tabasco in a saucepan. Mix well.
2. Bring the sauce to a boil, cover, lower the heat, and simmer for 20 minutes.

OLIVE SAUCE

2   teaspoons butter
2   teaspoons flour
⅓   cup milk
1   teaspoon Worcestershire sauce

5   stuffed olives, sliced
    Salt and freshly ground black
    pepper

1. Melt the butter in a small saucepan and stir in the flour. Then add the milk and keep stirring until the sauce begins to thicken.
2. Season the sauce with Worcestershire, sliced stuffed olives, and salt and pepper to taste. Taste the sauce and correct the seasonings, if necessary. Keep the sauce warm or reheat at serving time. Serve over poached chicken or fish, or as desired.

MADEIRA SAUCE

1 teaspoon butter	¼ cup canned beef gravy
½ clove minced garlic	1 teaspoon tomato purée
1 teaspoon minced shallots	½ teaspoon Worcestershire sauce
2 teaspoons Madeira	Salt and freshly ground black
1 teaspoon Burgundy	pepper

1. Melt the butter in a small heavy saucepan. Add the minced garlic and shallots, and brown lightly.
2. Add the Madeira and Burgundy and cook down over fairly high heat to about one half the original quantity.
3. Stir in the beef gravy, tomato purée, Worcestershire sauce, and salt and pepper to taste. Mix well and cook another minute or so. You can strain the sauce, or serve as is hot over fillet mignon or other beef or as you desire. This recipe makes about ¼ cup.

MUSHROOM SAUCE

2 teaspoons butter	2 teaspoons flour
1 teaspoon grated onion	Salt and freshly ground black
¼ cup peeled and sliced	pepper
mushrooms	¼ cup milk

1. Melt the butter in a saucepan with a cover and add the onion. Cook, stirring, for 1 minute, or until wilted. Add the sliced mushrooms. Stir and continue cooking over low heat for a minute or two longer.
2. Sprinkle the vegetables with flour, and add salt and pepper to taste. Mix well and pour the milk into the mixture all at once. Stir constantly until the sauce thickens. Cover and keep warm until serving time. Reheat if necessary.

SPICY TOMATO SAUCE

1 teaspoon butter	1 scallion, trimmed, washed, and
1 teaspoon flour	cut into fine dice including the
3 tablespoons hot water	green part
¼ teaspoon Worcestershire sauce	Salt and crushed red pepper
1 tablespoon tomato paste	flakes

1. Melt the butter and stir in the flour. Cook, stirring, for 1 minute and pour in the water. Stir until thickened.
2. Season with Worcestershire sauce, tomato paste, the scallion, and salt and crushed red pepper flakes to taste. Let stand until serving time. Heat and serve hot with meat loaf or other meat and vegetable dishes.

FRESH TOMATO SAUCE

2 teaspoons butter	¼ teaspoon dried thyme
1 tablespoon chopped onion	¼ teaspoon dried basil
1 medium-sized tomato, cored,	Salt and freshly ground black
peeled, and diced	pepper
¼ bay leaf	

1. Heat the butter in a small saucepan and add the chopped onion. Cook until wilted.
2. Add the tomato, bay leaf, thyme, basil, and salt and pepper to taste. Stir and cook for 10 minutes.
3. Blend the sauce in a food processor or pass it through a sieve and return it to the saucepan.
4. At serving time heat the sauce and serve hot over veal or spaghetti, or as you will.

TARTAR SAUCE

1 tablespoon mayonnaise
1 teaspoon sweet pickle relish
½ teaspoon Dijon mustard

1 teaspoon tarragon vinegar
3 stuffed olives, sliced

Mix all ingredients well and chill. Serve with oyster fritters and various fish.

Note: Many other ingredients are good in this quick and simple sauce. You can add capers, cucumber pickle, and parsley, to name just a few.

Eggs, Pizza, and Breads

Eggs are easily adapted to individual snacks and suppers, whether they are fried or scrambled, or served up more elegantly as Baked Eggs or a Grits and Cheese Soufflé. But, for an even greater change of pace, try my single-serving recipes for Pizza with Broccoli and Tuna, Cheese Pancakes, or tasty Butter Biscuits.

INDIVIDUAL QUICHE

Single crust for a 5-inch pie
(see recipe page 232)
1 slice bacon
1 small onion, peeled and thinly sliced
¼ cup Gruyere or Swiss cheese, cut into small cubes

1 egg, lightly beaten
3 tablespoons light cream
Pinch of nutmeg
Salt and freshly ground black pepper

1. Preheat the oven to 450 degrees.
2. Line a 5-inch pie plate with the crust and bake for 5 minutes. Set aside.
3. Cook the bacon until it is crisp. Remove the bacon and set it aside. Pour off most of the fat from the skillet and add the onion. Sauté until the onion is wilted, 1 or 2 minutes. Stir and separate the onion into rings.

4. Crumble the bacon and sprinkle the bits on the bottom of the pie crust. Top with sauteed onion and the cheese cubes.
5. In a small bowl, combine the egg, cream, and nutmeg with salt and pepper to taste. Mix well, beating the egg into the cream. Pour the mixture over the bacon and cheese in the pie crust.
6. Bake for 30 minutes, or until a knife inserted into the center of the filling comes out clean. Serve hot or cold.

BAKED EGGS

2 eggs
1 tablespoon butter
   Salt to taste

1 tablespoon cream, warmed in a Pyrex cup over a pilot light

1. Melt the butter in a ramekin. Break the eggs into the melted butter.
2. Using a Flame-Tamer, cook over low heat for 3 minutes.
3. Preheat the oven to 350 degrees.
4. Pour the warm cream over the egg yolks and finish cooking in the oven. Do not overcook. The yolks should be runny. Serve hot in the ramekin or on toast.

Note: Variations are numerous. Use almost any sauce, crumbs, tomatoes, potatoes, or other ingredients on top of the eggs or as a base for the eggs. Serve for breakfast or as a light lunch.

GRITS AND CHEESE SOUFFLE

½ cup milk	2 drops Tabasco
½ water	½ cup shredded Cheddar cheese
3 tablespoons white hominy grits	1 egg, separated
Pinch of nutmeg	Butter
Salt and freshly ground black pepper	

1. Combine the milk and water in a small saucepan with a cover. Bring to a boil, stir in the grits, cover, lower the heat, and cook for 15 minutes.
2. Preheat the oven to 350 degrees.
3. Season the grits with nutmeg and salt and pepper to taste. Stir well to mix in the seasonings. Add the egg yolk and half the cheese.
4. Beat the egg white until stiff.
5. Stir half the beaten egg white into the grits; then fold the remaining egg white carefully into the grits, using a spatula.
6. Pour the mixture into a small buttered soufflé dish. Top the soufflé with the remaining grated cheese and bake for 25 minutes. Serve warm for breakfast, lunch, or dinner.

INDIVIDUAL PIZZA

¼ cup flour	1 tablespoon lukewarm water
¼ teaspoon olive oil	Pinch of salt
½ teaspoon dry yeast	

1. Put the flour in a small bowl and add the olive oil. Stir slowly, pressing down on any lumps, until the mixture is smooth.
2. Dissolve the yeast in the water and add the mixture to the flour. Using the same spatula, stir and sweep the flour from the sides of the bowl into the dough, until a ball is formed. Cover the bowl with a paper towel and put it in a warm place for ½ hour, or until the dough rises.

3. Preheat the oven to 450 degrees.
4. Flour a sheet of wax paper or a bread board. Using your hands, knead the dough into a circle to fit your pan.
5. Pour a little oil into a 10-inch pie or pizza pan. Spread the oil over the pan.
6. Put the dough in the oiled pan and top it with any filling desired. Bake for 12 minutes, or until the filling is bubbling and the crust edges are crisp.

Note: Tomato, cheese, anchovies, mushrooms, olives, tuna, broccoli, and other partially-cooked vegetables, plus many other foods, may be used in infinite combinations for the filling. For this pie I start with ½ cup tomatoes and ½ cup cheese.

PIZZA WITH SAUSAGE

1 pizza dough (see recipe page 216)
Flour
1 link Italian sausage, cooked and thinly sliced
½ cup canned Italian-style plum tomatoes

2 teaspoons olive oil plus oil to grease the pan
Salt and freshly ground black pepper
2 tablespoons grated Parmesan cheese

1. Preheat the oven to 450 degrees.
2. Line a pie or pizza pan with aluminum foil. Spread a little oil over the foil.
3. Flour a sheet of wax paper and your hands and, using your hands, spread the dough in a circle on the wax paper. Transfer the dough to the prepared pan and continue to spread it out until the dough fits the pan.
4. Distribute the slices of sausage and the tomatoes evenly over the dough. Season the pizza with salt and pepper to taste and drip the oil over all. Top with grated cheese.
5. Bake for 12 minutes. Serve hot.

CHILI PIZZA

1 teaspoon dry yeast	½ cup flour
2 tablespoons, plus 1 teaspoon lukewarm water	2 teaspoons olive oil
	1½ cups chili (see recipe page 168)

1. Put the flour in a small bowl and add 1 teaspoon olive oil. Mix well, using a small rubber spatula.
2. Dissolve the yeast in the water and add it to the flour mixture. Stir to blend well. Scrape down the sides of the bowl to incorporate all the flour.
3. Work the dough into a compact mass and cover it with a cloth. Put the bowl in a warm place and let it rise for ½ hour.
4. Line a 10-inch pie or pizza pan with aluminum foil. Spread the foil with the remaining oil.
5. Preheat the oven to 350 degrees.
6. Flour your fingers and a flat surface and form the dough into a flat round. Put this in the center of the oiled and lined pan and continue to press and spread the dough to cover the bottom and sides of the pan. Let rest for 5 minutes.
7. Spread the dough with chili and bake for 15 minutes on the top shelf of the oven. Then move to the bottom shelf and bake for 10 minutes longer to cook the bottom crust. Test the side of the pizza for doneness and cook it a bit longer if you want a more crusty pizza. Serve hot.

PIZZA WITH BROCCOLI AND TUNA

1 small bunch broccoli
2 tablespoons olive oil
1 3½-ounce can tuna in oil
½ clove garlic, peeled and minced
Salt and freshly ground black pepper

½ cup flour
1 tablespoon butter, melted, plus butter to grease the pan
1 teaspoon sugar
½ teaspoon baking powder
1 egg

1. Separate and trim the broccoli flowerettes to bite-sized pieces. Leave 1 inch of stem on the flowerettes and discard the rest of the stems. Peel the stems.
2. Put the broccoli in a saucepan with a cover in water to cover, bring to a boil, cover, and simmer for 4 minutes. Drain the broccoli and put it into a small bowl. Add the olive oil, tuna, minced garlic, and salt and pepper to taste. Mix carefully.
3. Put the flour in a 5- or 6-inch bowl. Make a well in the flour and put the melted butter, sugar, baking powder, and egg into the well.
4. Using a spatula, gently incorporate the ingredients until a dough is formed. Knead the dough well and roll it out on a floured board or on floured wax paper to make a 6- to 8-inch round.
5. Preheat the oven to 350 degrees.
6. Line a 6- or 8-inch pan with aluminum foil and grease it well with butter. Fit the dough into the pan. Spread the filling on top of the dough and cover the pan with aluminum foil.
7. Bake for 30 minutes. Serve at room temperature. Any leftover pizza will be good the next day.

CHEESE PANCAKES

¼ cup milk
1 egg yolk
1 tablespoon butter, melted, plus enough to grease a griddle
¼ cup flour

½ teaspoon baking powder
½ teaspoon sugar
Pinch of salt
¼ cup shredded Cheddar or Gruyere cheese

1. Combine the milk, egg yolk, and butter in a small bowl. Beat well.
2. Combine the flour, baking powder, sugar, and salt in another bowl and add the milk mixture. Blend well and stir in the shredded cheese.
3. Grease a griddle, skillet, or crepe pan.
4. Pour half the batter onto the greased pan and cook over medium heat until the pancake is browned on both sides. Repeat with the remaining batter. This recipe will make two 5-inch pancakes, or more of a smaller size.

CORN BREAD

2 tablespoons cornmeal
1 teaspoon flour
1 teaspoon baking powder
¼ teaspoon sugar
⅛ teaspoon salt

1 egg yolk
2 tablespoons milk
1 tablespoon butter, melted
1 tablespoon minced hot cherry pepper

1. I use three small bowls or Pyrex muffin cups to prepare this. Put the butter in one and put it over the pilot light on your stove so that you will have melted butter when you need it. Mix the dry ingredients in another bowl. In the third bowl, mix the egg yolk, milk, and minced cherry pepper.

2. Preheat the oven to 400 degrees.
3. Pour the melted butter into the egg yolk/milk mixture. Then stir in the dry ingredients and blend well.
4. Spread the melted butter remaining in the first bowl all over the bowl. Then pour in the corn bread dough.
5. Bake for 25 minutes. Serve hot.

BUTTER BISCUITS

¼ cup flour, sifted	½ teaspoon sugar
¼ teaspoon salt	1 tablespoon butter
½ teaspoon baking powder	1 tablespoon milk

1. Sift the dry ingredients together into a small bowl.
2. Add the butter and mix well with your fingertips, until the mixture becomes grainy. Scrape the sides of the bowl to be sure that all the butter is incorporated.
3. Add the milk and continue mixing until a ball forms and the sides of the bowl are clean.
4. Preheat the oven to 400 degrees.
5. Separate the dough into 3 equal parts. Roll each between the palms of your hands to form balls.
6. Put the balls on a sheet of floured wax paper and, with floured hands, press the balls into rounds about ¼ inch thick. You can use a rolling pin, but it is not necessary for such a small quantity.
7. Bake for 10 minutes. Serve hot.

Sweets

Sometimes I am too full of other good food to top off a meal with an elaborate dessert. But I enjoy sweets and I like to do my own thing in this category from time to time. The perfect finish to a perfect meal can be as simple as a One-crust Fruit Pie or home-made Ice Cream, or as dramatic as Cherries Jubilee, Dorothy's Improved Chocolate Mousse, or Banana Flambée.

CHERRIES JUBILEE

1 teaspoon sugar
1 teaspoon cornstarch
¼ cup cherry juice
½ can (8¾ ounces) dark pitted cherries including the ¼ cup cherry juice

1 tablespoon kirsch or cognac
vanilla ice cream (optional)

1. Mix the sugar and cornstarch together in a small saucepan.
2. Measure ¼ cup juice out of the can of cherries and drain ½ the cherries and set aside.
3. Add the juice to the sugar and cornstarch mixture a little at a time, stirring constantly over low heat, until the sauce thickens, about 2 minutes.
4. Stir in the cherries.

5. At serving time, warm the liquor and pour it over the cherries and ignite it. Spoon the sauce over all cherries.
6. Serve over vanilla ice cream, if desired, or enjoy the sauce alone or with cake.

Note: The entire can of cherries may be used and the excess stored for a few days in the refrigerator. If so, double the other ingredients but cut down on the juice and liquor or the sauce might be too liquid. The remaining cherries, when you use only half the can, will go well with cereal.

APPLE PANCAKE

1 egg	1 teaspoon melted butter
2 tablespoons flour	Pinch of nutmeg
¼ teaspoon baking powder	1 tablespoon butter
1 teaspoon sugar	2 tablespoons sugar
Pinch of salt	1 pinch cinnamon
¼ cup milk	1 pinch nutmeg
¼ teaspoon vanilla	¼ apple, cored and thinly sliced

1. Blend egg, flour, baking powder, sugar and salt. Gradually add milk. Add the vanilla, melted butter, and nutmeg. Let stand while preparing the apple mixture.
2. Preheat the oven to 400 degrees.
3. Melt the 1 tablespoon butter in a small skillet and grease bottom and sides. Sprinkle the sugar, nutmeg, and cinnamon over the bottom of the skillet.
4. Distribute the apple slices evenly over the bottom of the skillet.
5. Pour the pancake batter over the apples and bring to a boil on top of the stove.
6. Bake for 15 minutes. Reduce the heat to 350 degrees and bake for another 15 minutes. Serve immediately.

POACHED PEAR WITH CHOCOLATE SAUCE

1 cup water
2 tablespoons sugar
1 pear, peeled, cored, and cut
   in half
¼ teaspoon vanilla extract
1 teaspoon butter

2 teaspoons cocoa
1 tablespoon sugar
1 teaspoon Karo syrup
1 tablespoon light cream
   Pinch of salt

1. Combine the water and sugar and bring to a boil. Add the pear halves and return to a boil. Reduce the heat and simmer, for about 5 minutes, or until the pear is tender to the touch of a fork.
2. Add the vanilla and let the pear cool in the syrup.
3. Mix the remaining ingredients well and heat to boiling. Cook for 1 minute and keep warm until serving time.
4. At serving time place the pear halves on a plate and cover with a tablespoon each of vanilla ice cream. Serve the hot chocolate sauce separately.

PEACH CRISP

3 tablespoons sugar
3 tablespoons flour
1 tablespoon butter
1 teaspoon lemon juice
   (optional)

1 peach, skinned or not, as
   desired
1 teaspoon grated lemon rind
   (optional)
   Pinch of cinnamon
   Pinch of nutmeg

1. Preheat the oven to 375 degrees.
2. Combine the sugar, flour, and butter and mix well, working butter into the flour and sugar as you would in making biscuits. Add the lemon juice and continue to mix and form a workable ball of dough. Pat the dough to a size to almost fit the baking dish.

3. Wash the peach well and cut it in half and remove the seed. Slice the peach and line the bottom of a greased baking dish with the peach slices. Sprinkle the slices with lemon rind, if desired.
4. Lay the dough over the peach slices and sprinkle with cinnamon and nutmeg. Bake for ½ hour. Serve hot or cold with cream or vanilla ice cream.

APPLE CRISP

¼ cup brown sugar
3 tablespoons flour
1 tablespoon butter
Pinch of cinnamon
Pinch of nutmeg

1 cooking apple, peeled, cored, and thinly sliced
¼ teaspoon grated lemon rind (optional)
1 teaspoon lemon juice (optional)

1. Preheat the oven to 375 degrees.
2. Combine the sugar, flour, and butter and blend together. Add the cinnamon and nutmeg. Stir in the lemon rind and juice, if desired.
3. Put the apple slices in the bottom of a greased ovenproof dish.
4. Pour the dough mixture over the apples and bake, uncovered, for ½ hour. Serve hot or cold with vanilla ice cream on top.

BANANE FLAMBEE

1 medium-sized banana	2 tablespoons sherry
1 teaspoon butter	2 shakes nutmeg
2 tablespoons honey	1 shake cinnamon
2 tablespoons fresh orange juice	1 tablespoon light rum

1. Peel the banana and split it in half lengthwise.
2. Melt the butter in a skillet or flameproof baking dish and add the banana halves.
3. Mix the honey, orange juice, sherry, and spices together.
4. Preheat the oven to 400 degrees.
5. Pour the honey mixture over the banana halves and bake for 15 minutes.
6. Remove the bananas from the oven and pour the rum over them. Ignite the rum and, when the flame dies, serve the bananas with the warm sauce.

DOROTHY'S IMPROVED CHOCOLATE MOUSSE

2 tablespoons sugar	1 teaspoon black coffee or ¼ teaspoon instant coffee dissolved in 1 teaspoon hot water
1 tablespoon water	
2 tablespoons Droste's cocoa or 1 ounce unsweetened chocolate	
1 egg, separated	¼ teaspoon vanilla extract
	Pinch of cream of tartar

1. Dissolve 1 tablespoon sugar in 1 tablespoon water and bring the mixture to a boil.
2. Place the cocoa in a bowl or melt the Baker's chocolate and place it in the bowl and stir in the boiling sugar water mixture.
3. Add to the chocolate mixture the egg yolk, coffee, and vanilla. Mix well.

4. Beat the egg white and cream of tartar until stiff. Add the remaining tablespoon of sugar to the beaten egg white.
5. Mix one-half of the beaten egg white into the chocolate mixture; carefully fold in the remaining beaten egg white. It need not be completely incorporated, a marbled look is interesting.
6. Refrigerate the mousse for at least 1 hour before serving.

CHRISTMAS CUSTARD DESSERT

This sauce is delicious by itself, but it was such fun as a child to add a teaspoon of good bourbon whisky at the table, passing the bottle under the acute scrutiny of Aunt Sallie.

1 egg yolk	½ cup milk
1 tablespoon sugar	3 drops vanilla extract
Pinch of salt	

1. In a small bowl, beat the egg yolk and sugar together with a wire whisk until well incorporated. Beat in the salt. Pour the mixture into the top of a double boiler.
2. Scald the milk and pour it and the vanilla into the egg, sugar, and salt mixture, stirring constantly with a whisk over barely simmering water. Cook until the sauce begins to thicken slightly. It will not become really thick but the consistency of a sauce to be eaten with a spoon. Refrigerate for several hours.

Note: You can top the custard with whipped cream, if you want.

BREAD PUDDING

½ cup bread crumbs or ½ slice of trimmed bread in crumbs
1 cup milk
1 egg lightly beaten

2 tablespoons sugar
Pinch of cinnamon
Pinch of nutmeg

1. Soak the bread crumbs in the milk for 20 minutes at least.
2. Heat the oven to 350 degrees.
3. Grease a small casserole. Add the sugar, spices, and egg to the bread and milk mixture. Mix well.
4. Pour the pudding into the greased casserole and bake for 40 minutes, or until firm on top.

ICE CREAM

½ pint heavy cream
¼ cup sugar
1 teaspoon vanilla extract

Pinch of salt
Dash of almond extract

Place all ingredients in the container of an ice cream freezer made to fit the freezer compartment of your refrigerator. Shut the refrigerator door on the cord and plug it into the electric current. Let the churning and freezing progress until the sound indicates the paddles are laboring. Turn off the current. Serve reasonably soon or before ice crystals form.

Serve with one of these sauces:
Grated bitter chocolate and crème de menthe
Raspberry, apricot, or peach preserves
Chestnut pieces or sauce
Maple syrup and pecans
Chocolate sauce
Butterscotch sauce

DATE CAKE

4 dates, pitted and chopped	1 tablespoon brown sugar
2 teaspoons brandy	¼ teaspoon baking powder
2 tablespoons flour	Pinch of salt
1 egg	Butter to grease the baking pan

1. Preheat the oven to 350 degrees.
2. Put the chopped dates in a very small cup and pour the brandy over them. Mix well and let stand for at least ½ hour.
3. In a small mixing bowl beat the flour, egg, brown sugar, baking powder, and salt until the flour is incorporated and all lumps are dissolved.
4. Add the chopped dates and brandy and stir again. Mix well and pour into a buttered 5-inch pie tin or a Pyrex muffin cup. Bake for 20 minutes or until a knife inserted in the center comes out clean.

MERINGUES

1 egg white	2 drops vanilla extract
Pinch of salt	2 drops almond extract
¼ cup sugar	(optional)

1. Put the egg white in a small pyrex bowl and beat with your electric beater, using just one of the two rotaries. Beat until the white is stiff and will form peaks.
2. Continue beating and add the sugar a little at a time. Add the flavorings.
3. Preheat the oven to 250 degrees.
4. Line a baking sheet with aluminum foil and brush it lightly with butter to prevent sticking. Drop large spoonfuls on the sheet and bake for 1 hour. Yield: 3 or 4 depending on the drop. Serve with ice cream and a sauce or try one alone.

STRAWBERRY SHORTCAKE

¼ cup flour
½ teaspoon baking powder
   Salt to taste
1½ teaspoons sugar
1 teaspoon butter

3 teaspoons milk
⅔ cup sliced strawberries
   Cream or whipped cream to
   top the cake

1. Sift the flour, baking powder, salt, and ½ teaspoon sugar into a small mixing bowl. Add the butter.
2. Cut in the butter with a knife and, finally, with your fingers to thoroughly incorporate the shortening in the flour mixture.
3. Add the milk and stir until you can form a ball. Flour the fingers and pick up the dough and knead it for a few minutes on floured wax paper. Roll it out on the floured paper and shape two small crusts by hand for the two layers of shortcake. Put the layers on a sheet of aluminum foil.
4. Preheat the oven to 450 degrees.
5. Bake for 12 minutes, or until done.
6. Sprinkle the sliced strawberries with the remaining sugar, mix, and let set for ½ hour or so.
7. Place one crust on a plate and cover with half the berries. Top with the other crust and add the remaining berries. Serve with cream, whipped cream, or ice cream.

Note: Other fruits, such as cherries and peaches, can be substituted for the strawberries.

PIE CRUST

This will make a 7-inch single crust or top and bottom crust for a smaller pie or a small baking-dish cobbler.

½ cup sifted flour
2 tablespoons plus 1 teaspoon
    vegetable shortening

1 tablespoon plus 1 teaspoon
    cold water
    Pinch of salt

1. Mix flour, salt, and shortening in a small bowl using your finger tips. Continue mixing until it is grainy in texture. Or use a food processor, turning the motor on and off several times until the mixture is grainy.
2. Add 1 tablespoon cold water, then 1 teaspoon. Form the dough into a ball. This will happen automatically in the food processor. Refrigerate the dough for at least ½ hour. Then knead it by hand.
3. Flour a sheet of wax paper and roll out the dough to fit the pie pan or baking dish.
4. Preheat the oven to 400 degrees.
5. Bake for 30 minutes filled with your favorite fruit filling. For a pie shell without filling bake at 500 degrees for 12 minutes.

Note: It is difficult to transfer the rolled out dough to the pie pan. Try using a pancake turner and if the transfer is not perfect, patch the bare spot or spots and press into the pan. It will still taste good.

APPLE PIE

1 pie crust (see recipe above)
    rolled out to fit the pan
1 apple, cored and sliced
3 tablespoons brown sugar

2 teaspoons cornstarch
1 tablespoon water
2 teaspoons butter

1. Preheat the oven to 400 degrees.
2. Put the apple slices on the bottom of the pie crust dough in the pie pan and sprinkle with the brown sugar.
3. Blend the cornstarch and water and pour over the apple slices. Dot with butter. Bake for 30 minutes.

Note: Use any fruit you want in the same manner varying the sweetener, as desired, from brown to white sugar or honey.

ONE-CRUST FRUIT PIE

This will make enough crust for a 5-inch pie tin.

¼ cup sifted flour	1 tablespoon shortening
Pinch of salt	2 teaspoons ice water

1. Put flour, salt and shortening in the container of a food processor or blender and blend for 1 or so minutes. Scrape down the sides of the container, cover and blend a minute or so longer or until the flour mixture is grainy. Add the water 1 teaspoon at a time and blend in between. Use only the amount of water needed to produce a dough that can be gathered into a ball. Omit the second teaspoon of water if not needed. Refrigerate the dough briefly. To mix by hand, put the first 3 ingredients in a bowl and mix with the fingertips to attain the grainy state. Add the water slowly and continue working to form the ball of dough.
2. Flour a sheet of wax paper and roll the dough out in a round shape about ⅛ inch thick. Put the dough in the pie tin and fit it to the bottom and sides. Cut off the excess hanging over the sides of the pan. Using a knife, dull side, make indentations in the crust around the edge to improve the appearance. Any scraps of dough may be rolled out to make strips of dough for the top of the pie if desired. Otherwise, discard the excess or use it to patch if necessary. Refrigerate the crust in the tin.

FILLINGS FOR ONE-CRUST PIES

10 or 12 bing cherries, pitted and sliced in half

1 very ripe peach, peeled, pitted and sliced

1 small apple, peeled, cored, and sliced

8 or 9 strawberries, hulled, washed, and sliced

¼ cup blueberries, picked over, washed, and crushed

1 ripe pear, peeled, cored, and sliced

¼ cup or so of any fruit you fancy, pared and seeded and sliced

2 teaspoons sugar, or to taste, depending on the ripeness of the fruit

½ teaspoon cornstarch

1. Place one of the above fruits in a small saucepan over low heat. Stir well.
2. Mix the sugar and cornstarch in a small bowl. Stir the sugar and cornstarch into the simmering fruit and cook for 1 minute.
3. Remove the pie crust from the refrigerator and pour in the warm fruit mixture. Place the strips of dough across the top of the pie, if desired.
4. Bake at 400 degrees for 30 minutes.

PECAN PIE

2 tablespoons dark Karo syrup

1 tablespoon sugar

1 egg

10 whole pecans

1 tablespoon melted butter

1 pie crust (see recipe page 232)

1. Preheat the oven to 350 degrees.
2. Shake the syrup to mix it well and portion out 2 tablespoons into a small mixing bowl.
3. Mix in the sugar and the egg. Blend well.
4. Incorporate the pecans and the melted butter into the filling and pour the mixture into the pie crust.
5. Bake for 30 minutes.

Index